D1600329

By the same author

Theology and the Arts
The Ambiguity of Religion
Grace and Common Life
Faith and Virtue
Images for Self-Recognition
Creed and Personal Identity

Patience

Patience

How We Wait Upon the World

David Baily Harned

WIPF & STOCK · Eugene, Oregon

Wipf and Stock Publishers
199 W 8th Ave, Suite 3
Eugene, OR 97401

Patience
How We Wait Upon the World
By Harned, David Baily and Hein, David

ISBN 13: 978-1-4982-1758-3
Publication date 1/15/2015
Previously published by Cowley Publications, 1997

For Elaine,
who makes all things worthwhile

Contents

Acknowledgments

This manuscript was written in London at Sion College. My windows overlooked the Thames, where I could watch boats dancing with the current or else slowly and patiently struggling against the tide toward Richmond or Greenwich or beyond. I am much indebted to the librarian and assistant librarian at Sion, Stephen Gregory and Georgette Stavrou, for their friendship and counsel and unfailing good humor. I am also much indebted to the administrator of the College, my friend Major General John C. Hardy, who gave up his own office so that I could have a place to work undisturbed during the last months before Sion College left its Victorian premises on the Embankment for more modest quarters in the neighborhood. I was the last person to use the old building, and I am deeply grateful for the privilege.

In this country I owe particular thanks to five people: Professor David Hein of Hood College, who has been so generous with advice and support for more than a quarter of a century; Professor Edward H. Henderson, chairman of the department of Philosophy and Religious Studies at Louisiana

State University, for his encouragement and careful reading of the manuscript; and Professor Carolyn H. Hargrave, former Provost of LSU, who invited me to the university and whose gift of friendship has been an unfailing support. As always, I am grateful to Professor Nathan A. Scott, Jr., of the University of Virginia, the best of friends. Finally, I am indebted to Cynthia Shattuck, director of Cowley Publications. She is an editor both rigorous and understanding; this book has benefited very much from her thoughtful suggestions.

— David Baily Harned
Baton Rouge, Louisiana

Foreword

In his latest book David Harned is sounding a new note in the field of moral theology, for, despite the persuasiveness with which such people as Alasdair MacIntyre and Gilbert Meilaender have reinstated theory of virtue in contemporary discussion, the theological forum today remains largely silent about the particular virtue which Harned so eloquently bids us to reconsider—namely, the virtue of patience.

In an elaborately intricate but always lucid argument he reviews the biblical tradition, early Christian theological tradition (Tertullian, Lactantius, Cyprian, Augustine, Gregory I), the medieval line of Aquinas and Thomas à Kempis, such Protestant voices as Luther and Calvin and Jonathan Edwards, and the testimony of a variety of modern theologians. And what he most wants to disclose is the consistency with which Christian thought across the centuries has conceived patience to be not a secondary virtue, but indispensable for the realization of any virtue at all.

Though he has produced a brilliant essay in formal theology, his book is so beautifully written that it moves the heart and (like that armchair torso of Apollo in Rilke's famous poem) bids us to "change your life."

— *Nathan A. Scott, Jr.*
William R. Kenan Professor Emeritus of Religious Studies and Professor Emeritus of English at the University of Virginia

Chapter One

The Loss of Patience

why wait?

Less than forty years ago a dictionary of Christian ethics was published by the press of one of the church's major and most literate denominations. It was edited by an eminent theologian and its eighty contributors from various religious communities were drawn equally from both sides of the Atlantic. The dictionary contained entries on pessimism, pleasure, polygamy, prostitution, and propaganda, but there was no listing for patience. Nor was patience mentioned in the very brief entry devoted to virtue. The omission was not an accident, for in a much later and revised edition it was not rectified. The neglect of patience would be all the more remarkable if the dictionary were not a fair reflection of the theological and cultural temper of its time and of our own.

In the course of a century and a quarter, scarcely a handful of books in Christian theology and ethics written in English have been devoted to the importance of patience. Because the virtue has continued to receive some attention in literary and

historical studies, its absence from Christian reflection is puzzling. By and large, a rich and complex idea that was consistently employed for almost two thousand years to represent the highest possibilities of human life, both in the classical and the Christian traditions, has been allowed to wither away. The church appears to have lost, or at least mislaid for a great many years, some of its patrimony. What does the loss of patience mean for the assumptions it once enshrined about God, the world and time, the self and its relationships? What does it suggest about the assumptions that now govern our own thoughts and actions?

By the middle of the nineteenth century, it seemed that every old regime and old assurance had been threatened by the corrosion of modernity. The voices proclaiming that God had emigrated to a foreign land were not so much prophets as chroniclers of a new age already begun. By 1848—the year of revolution which saw not only the publication of *The Communist Manifesto* but also sporadic uprisings throughout Europe—the idea of patience had virtually disappeared as an independent topic in Christian literature published in the English-speaking world. Social problems without precedent and the promise of a brave new world, both legacies of the industrial revolution, as well as changed cultural assumptions and new directions in theology, all conspired in the discrediting of patience. The virtue came to be seen either as an anachronism or as a notion devised by oppressors to contain the restlessness and discontent of the oppressed. The idea of patience survived, of course, but in its tamed and domesticated form as a mere convention of civilized interchange it meant far less than it had as an integral part of a living religious tradition. As early as the eighteenth century, Alasdair MacIntyre writes in *After Virtue*, the linkage of patience and hope had become obscure, so that hope was deferred to the next life and patience

enjoined in this life because it was otherwise hopeless. In its diminished state, patience came to signify precisely the reverse of what it had originally represented: a person's triumph over all the diversions and afflictions that can test our powers of endurance, forbearance, and discipline.

With the onset of modernity, furthermore, there were many who believed that Christianity had valued the endurance of suffering more than it had struggled to relieve it, and that suffering more often drugged sinners than brought them to repentance. Faith in progress and the possibilities of radical social change captured the imaginations of Christians and secularists alike. Insofar as patience meant the uncomplaining endurance of adversity, it frequently seemed childlike in no very admirable sense—an unimaginative failure of nerve. And if the worth of the virtue had become problematical, the larger question was not what importance patience still retained as a key for interpreting the mysteries of God's nature and ways with his creation, but whether the inherited doctrines of God, providence, the person and work of Christ, and eschatology exercised their powers of persuasion in what seemed like a different world. So its virtual disappearance from Christian discourse was simply the consequence of interest in other issues as well as the sense that many traditional ideas urgently required revision. Christianity's exhortations to patience in the social and political realms left the church vulnerable to accusations that it was ideological and reactionary.

As mere surrender, for example, patience seemed no more than immature reluctance to face the daunting tasks of refashioning and perfecting a still unfinished world. Separated from the rich context afforded by the disclosure of God's nature in his mighty acts, the obedience of Christ, and the reciprocity and responsiveness that life in community involves, it is small wonder that patience seems to have lost its power to reconcile

and heal and comfort. In its truncated and withered form the virtue has been isolated from both theology and common experience—not to mention common sense. We must explore the magnitude of this loss and the extent to which it can distort what the church has to say to the world today. First, however, we must examine several basic assumptions that seem to characterize our day and distinguish it from earlier times.

It would be difficult for many of us to agree that "the decision to wait is one of the great human acts."[1] For scores of previous generations, however, and especially for those who were touched by the claims of the Christian message, the truth of the statement was beyond dispute. How else can we allow the future to emerge? The patience that waiting entailed was a great human act because it summoned the most distinctive powers of the self to their finest expression—vision and imagination, faith and hope, courage and prudence, humility and love.

Today waiting remains no less a part of our lives than it ever was for our ancestors. But our assumptions about human nature and fulfillment have changed, and therefore our attitude toward waiting has changed as well. We see it less often as an opportunity, more often as a diminishing of the quality of our lives, a deprivation enforced upon us by an unfriendly environment. If reality can be more or less equated with everything we can manipulate and control, then does not the need to wait suggest a failure in ourselves? We have not yet found our place in the sun, nor achieved the mastery of our surroundings. Far from being one of the great human acts, waiting simply testifies that we have not won our struggle with

the world. It tells us less about our strength than our weakness and lack of invention.

Therefore waiting means there are voids in our universe, holes and tatters in what is intended to be the seamless fabric of our activity, and so we must do something with these empty spaces. They must be filled. If they are not, we shall become anxious or bored, which is the matrix for all sorts of destructive behavior toward others and toward oneself. If waiting is pointless, where can it end except in boredom unless it is relieved? The name of such relief is busyness, which might be described uncharitably as endless activity without an end in view. Busyness is important for two reasons. First, it is a distraction, diverting our attention from the need to wait, and so it contributes mightily to our self-esteem in a world where human significance is equated with doing things. God forbid that we should go to our death without keeping busy every step of the way—otherwise we will have squandered our allotted time. By keeping busy we will have no time to reflect on what a strange inversion of the contemplative Christian tradition this is.

The second reason is the role of busyness in expressing an impulse deeply written into our culture: the desire to believe that, no matter what, everything is all right. Busyness allows us to forget that the ordinary course of human affairs involves the sapping of our energy, our growing dependence upon the kindness of others, the inevitability of waiting, and yielding to forces far stronger than our own. In the end, what keeping busy means is quite simply the refusal, sometimes very brave and sometimes thoughtless, to look reality in the face. But this is also to turn from God, who is the ultimate reality, and especially from Jesus Christ and the narrative of his passion, with its constant focus upon patience and vulnerability, suffering and passivity.

We have touched upon two pervasive assumptions of our impatient age that require further exploration. The first is that waiting is not at the core and center of human life but somehow *accidental:* we should not have to wait. Human progress should

mean our emancipation from the necessity to wait, because science and technology have freed us from so many forms of dependence upon our natural environment. In fact, however, affluence and inventiveness have not so much reduced our time spent waiting as simply changed it: fast cars speed into gridlock. Advances in medicine increase our dependence upon others and the time we spend waiting for their attention, because greater longevity usually involves some loss of self-sufficiency. Transportation technology has played a dramatic role in transforming the world into a global village—which means not only greater speed but more crowded skies, more crowded planes, more delays, and more time squandered waiting in the air and on the ground.

For all of us some of the time, and for some of us all of the time, the experience of waiting remains our daily bread. A recent study claimed that the average person spends eleven or more days each year waiting in line, but this only begins to sketch the proportions of waiting. It is the most familiar aspect of our lives: we wait for the mail, for a telephone call, for a plane or train or taxi in the rain, for this appointment or that, for a human voice after an electronic system has delivered its menu of fifteen options we do not want. We wait for red lights and congested traffic, for relief of pain and for the restoration of health, for help or for attention, for hurts to heal and embarrassments to be forgotten. Waiting is not accidental, something that might have been avoided by more careful planning or greater influence or affluence.

In *The Stature of Waiting,* British theologian W. H. Vanstone argues for radical revision of the commonplace view that we have achieved a mastery over the environment of which earlier generations never dreamed. On the contrary, because of our complex technical and organizational systems, he argues, waiting will become an ever larger part of our lives:

> The social and economic organization of the Western world is developing in such a way that, in ever-increasing areas and phases of life, the individual is cast in the role of patient, of recipient rather than achiever, of one who must wait and depend on factors outside his control.... Perhaps the transition of the individual into a condition of ever more marked dependence or receptivity or passion is, for the foreseeable future, irreversible.[2]

There is little reason to believe that waiting is less appropriate today than it was generations ago as a mark of the human condition. It is not an incidental and peripheral element in human life but one of its perennial and most revelatory aspects. It is different for us, however, because we have learned to dominate our natural environment in ways that our ancestors could never even contemplate. This has fostered expectations that social realities all too often refuse to honor, for our social context is not amenable to control in the same way as is the natural world. And this disparity breeds endless frustration, discontent, and impatience.

The second dubious assumption that we have to address is that "real life" is activity, agency, getting things done. We assume we are most fully human when we are in control, actors and not acted upon, subjects rather than objects. So one aspect of life is devalued and juxtaposed to another, as in the *Oxford English Dictionary's* definition of agency as "acting, exerting power, producing an effect, as opposed to patient." What matters is what we accomplish, not what we are given. There are many powerful reasons to believe that doing things represents what is finest and most satisfying in human life. Little could seem more obvious than the satisfactions of founding one's own company, or rapid promotion in a large organization, or amassing great wealth and

using it for humane and charitable ends. But if human fulfillment must be identified with action and inventiveness, with the exercise of power and a thirst for competition, with achieving mastery and control, then it is to our discredit if we are dependent upon others, if we cannot earn our daily bread, if we become infirm and incapable, if we are not always engaged in some useful activity.

This notion that earlier generations described by the words *homo faber*, "man the maker," divides humanity into two camps: those who have realized their potential and all the others who have not, or do not, or will no longer, and whose only real busyness lies in squandering what their lives were intended to be. Unemployment, which is endemic to any postindustrial society, becomes a spiritual crisis and not simply an economic problem. For if we are essentially workers and valued only in terms of our social utility, then exclusion from the community of achievers means that the self is alienated from its own true nature. What grounds remain for self-esteem, except whatever comfort memories afford? Unemployment means that we are temporarily banished from the world of meaning and morality.

Is this assumption valid, that in some profound sense we are little else than what we have achieved? What if our greatest significance lay instead in our involvement in the lives of others? And what if this involvement did not mean our power to form them but our responsiveness and receptivity to them, our willingness to step back when appropriate and give them room? There is good reason to heed Vanstone's counsel, "It is not necessarily the case that man is most fully human when he is achiever rather than receiver, active rather than passive, subject rather than object of what is happening."[3] What if we are most fully human when we receive, not when we achieve? Perhaps the source of human dignity lies elsewhere than in our works.

There has been no finer defense of the contemplative ideal than *Leisure: The Basis of Culture* by Josef Pieper. This eminent Roman Catholic philosopher argues that the value we place on agency and productivity and busyness represents a radical departure from the classical assumptions that previously shaped society. Today the very idea of leisure has become suspect, for if the truly happy person is one who lives for his or her work, leisure has dubious value—unless it is a time of necessary relaxation and renewal to enhance our productivity. For Pieper, however, the real meaning of leisure has little connection with what we do when the day's work is finished. It is not synonymous with weekends, "spare" time or "free" time, vacations or holidays, all of which can be filled with a ceaseless round of activities; such exercises are really very little different from work itself. Leisure does not denote merely a void or a hole in our schedule that we can fill as we like. In fact, we no longer know what it means.

What, then, is leisure? Pieper argues that we must understand it not as a quantity of time but as a quality of mind, not as an hour or a day but as a kind of waiting. Inactive men and women may have no leisure at all, while committed and active people may have it in abundance. Leisure is, he writes, "an attitude of the mind, a condition of the soul, and as such utterly contrary to the ideal of 'worker.'" It implies

> an attitude of non-activity, of inward calm, of silence; it means not being "busy," but letting things happen. Leisure is a form of silence, of that silence which is a prerequisite of the apprehension of reality.... The soul's power to "answer" to the reality of the world is left undisturbed.[4]

Leisure means waiting upon the world. It has the appearance of "doing nothing" because it is passivity in the particular sense of receptivity, alert and vigilant suffering, responsiveness to what is truly other, *theoria* instead of *praxis*, grateful contemplation. So leisure has to do with knowing—knowing the secrets of things and

their inherent intelligibility. It means pausing, leaving behind all the problems of the everyday world in order to focus upon mysteries, joyfully and with eyes filled with wonder. Leisure is concerned with vision, imagination, empathy, and poetry. Thus patience must always lie at the center of leisure, for reality does not disclose its secrets to careless, hasty, or indifferent scrutiny.

Pieper contends there can be no true leisure apart from faith in God. How could we be playful, unserious for a moment, uninvolved in all the world's affairs, if the whole weight of everything whatsoever falls on our own shoulders? "Cut off from the worship of the divine," Pieper writes, "leisure becomes laziness and work inhuman.... The opportunity is given for the mere killing of time, and for boredom with its marked similarity to the inability to enjoy leisure."[5] The ceaseless activity that is so often the other side of our incapacity to enjoy leisure has its source, strange as it initially may seem, in impatience and laziness, in the sloth which—as one of the seven deadly sins—is the origin of a multitude of sins beyond itself.

An older and less familiar name for sloth is *acedia*, a failing that was long regarded as a particular peril for monastic communities. *Acedia* signifies a distaste for well-being and well-doing that expresses itself either in withdrawal from others or else in relentless busyness that enables the self to hide from itself. They are two sides of the same coin. At the height of the Middle Ages, Pieper tells us, sloth and restlessness, "leisurelessness," the incapacity to enjoy leisure, were closely connected:

> Sloth was held to be the source of restlessness, and the ultimate cause of "work for work's sake."... Idleness, in the medieval view, means that a man prefers to forgo the rights, or if you prefer the claims, that belong to his nature. In a word, he does not want to be as God wants him to be, and

> that ultimately means that he does not wish to be what he really, fundamentally, *is*.[6]

The cure for *acedia* cannot be found anywhere within the fallen world of work, for the busyness there is so frequently a symptom for the disease itself. Impatience and busyness and boredom—so commonplace and yet the guises of deadly sin and the sources of myriad other sins. Not in modern activism but only in the virtue of patience, if older scholars were correct, can a true remedy be discovered: the gift of perseverance, exercised in the service of

waiting upon the world.

Perhaps the greatest of our problems, apart from our inability to value ourselves except in terms of our social utility and the rewards it brings, is that we can enjoy only what we have earned with great effort. We cannot receive anything as a gift, with a good conscience. In other words, we refuse to be "patients." But are we then fated never to understand the meaning of the Christian faith? Such is Pieper's view, for grace means that "everything gained and everything claimed follows upon something given, and comes after something gratuitous and unearned."[7] If we cannot accept a gift, then what reason is there ever to express gratitude, except in the minimal sense of the acknowledgment of a just wage in an unjust world? But does not Christianity mean, first of all, the acceptance of gifts, and is not gratitude the chief motivation for the Christian life?

In Pieper's eyes, there can be little doubt that many of the fundamental assumptions of contemporary society—that the process of growth and development is a passage from passivity to activity, that passivity is infantile and unrewarding, that doing something is always better than doing nothing, that work provides the meaning and justification for our existence—are not only different from those of the Christian tradition but hostile to it and in some instances a complete reversal of it. Restlessness and laziness, impatience and boredom and despair, busyness that is the

flight of the self from itself—all of these are the adversaries of patience. All of them are unprepared to wait upon the world: to pay attention, to listen carefully rather than to speak, to accept quietude and stillness, to enjoy mysteries and wonders, to accept the suffering, patience, and humility that are fitting responses to the world's otherness and variety. That is the secret contemplation can teach. It sharpens our capacity to be affected, to bear willingly the imprint of what happens outside ourselves, to stand in someone else's shoes, to listen to others before we try to shape them to our own desires.

If there is enduring value in the contemplative tradition, is it not also true that assertions about the preeminence of activity are based on a distinction between "active" and "passive" that is remote from ordinary life? In fact, passivity can be a profound act of the self when, for example, it means willingness to share in the anguish of someone else in silent companionship. What is opposed to such sensitivity or empathy is not action but indifference or lack of feeling. Most simply, silence can often speak more loudly than a cry and accomplish far more good. Doing nothing can be a more creative act and a greater achievement than doing anything at all—and it can require far more strength, selflessness, and courage.

The refusal to exercise one's own initiative too quickly can also provide others with time and space to realize their own possibilities for growth. Turning aside a plea for help from a frustrated child can encourage him or her to achieve a new measure of independence and forsake childish ways. Parents will corrupt the development of their offspring if they are not able to refrain from acting, and by such restraint encourage their children to accept appropriate risks, test their own strength, grow more self-reliant. Keeping silence in the face of unjust accusations or unwarranted anger may be the most difficult course of action possible, but it may also create the

potential for reconciliation where otherwise there would be nothing but endless recrimination. Refraining from intervention in a dispute among other people may give them time to come to a satisfactory resolution of the affair when any other action, no matter how well-informed or well-intended, would be seen as a diversion or a meddlesome intrusion.

In other words, apparent passivity, waiting, yielding, accepting, silence, and similar responses, are not necessarily disclosures of weakness or cause for shame, signs that we have failed to become all that we were intended to be. All of these are aspects of the idea of suffering, in its fundamental sense as empathy, responsiveness to the presence of others, mutuality and dialogue, accepting the initiatives of other people as a part of life together, relationships of caring and responsibility and love. All of these are acts of patience. Sometimes they are thrust upon us and sometimes they are deliberately sought out, but they are all among the most significant and creative acts that we can ever undertake because of the ways they can exercise transformative power in the lives of others. The decision *not* to act can be the most helpful act of which we are capable. Such patience is not the surrender of our initiative but often its wisest expression, because it invites and supports the initiative of others. Then perhaps a dry seed will burst into a blossom whose luxuriance the solitary individual could never have envisioned.

So passivity and activity are inextricably bound up with one another. They do not represent a movement from childhood to maturity, or the difference between a life of little worth and one that is truly memorable and satisfying. Our freedom to act develops as we respond to the initiatives of other people. It is a mistake to identify human excellence with our activities; our ability to react and respond plays no less of a part. The ways that we can suffer distinguish us from all other creatures as much as the initiatives we undertake. Our creativity emerges from the interaction between the range and richness of our sensitivity and the caring and claims

and independence of our neighbors. Everything depends upon the imagination with which we exercise the freedom that others have shaped for us and that we could never have discovered if we were invulnerable, separate continents, independent states. So it must be if our existence means interdependence and mutuality, and if its basic unit is not the solitary individual, but two persons interacting. History books may recount the extraordinary deeds of individuals, but the two fundamental sources of our knowledge of what it means to be human—the family or extended household and the games a child learns to play with others—both testify beyond dispute that life is life together, a thoroughly dialogical and relational affair.

Waiting is not an accidental part of life together, but lies at the center of things. Nor is it evidence of human weakness, or an emptiness that we must struggle to fill. How could we hold the simplest conversation if we were not willing to wait for the other to speak? Sometimes waiting offers a needed respite, a chance to regain our strength, or to see where we are. Sometimes it is exhilarating, when we can look forward to a friend's return, or a long-awaited trip, or a deserved vacation. Waiting for things can often make them better; anticipation endows the world with new luster and richness. Life would quickly grow stale and tedious if there were never a need to wait. What is most important, however, is the recognition that waiting is at the center of things not because of the nature of the world, not because of the nature of society, but because of who we are—made to be dependent, incomplete in isolation from others.

We have also seen that "real life" cannot be equated with acts and initiatives; inaction and responsiveness are no less important. Life is conversation, and in our speech with one another each has its essential role to play. The tendency to value one more than the other is foreign to their actual

interdependence. Keeping silence, or enduring what could be avoided, or refraining from punishment where punishment is due, or choosing not to intervene, though they appear to be no actions at all, can produce effects of far-reaching importance.

Finally, it is important to stress that neglecting the crucial role of patience, vulnerability, and waiting also challenges some fundamental elements in the Christian tradition. Surely one of the first lessons to be gleaned from the passion of Jesus is that we are most like God not in our independence but in our dependence, not in our transformation of the world but in our capacity to drink to the lees the cup of suffering it offers, not in expressing our own initiatives but in waiting upon the initiatives of others. As the last days of Jesus attest, so Vanstone writes, God discloses himself and exercises his sovereignty precisely when he subjects himself to the world. In loving the world, God "gives to the world the terrible power to have meaning to and for Himself. So He...waits upon the world, exposed to and receptive of its power of meaning. In all the history of the world, *Deus, qui non passibilis, passus est.*"[8] To discover the meaning of the *imago dei*, what humanity is intended to be, we have the biblical portrait of the suffering Christ. From this perspective, it is evident that the image of a God who is engaged with his world involves both activity and exposure. A person, writes Vanstone,

> must not see it as degrading that he should wait upon the world, be helped, be provided for, be dependent, for as such he is, by God's gift, what God Himself makes Himself to be. That man is made, by God's gift, to know and feel his dependence on the world is no less a mark of God's image in him than that he is made, also by God's gift, to know and feel his capacity for acting and achieving.[9]

If the image of God has something fundamental to do with passivity and waiting, with being a patient, then there is urgent reason to reassess the virtue from a Christian perspective, especially after such a long period of neglect.

Conventional notions of patience today, however, can lead us far away from what it has meant in the Christian tradition. When a tradition comes to be perceived as outdated, its power spent and its counsel irrelevant, it does not quickly die. For better and for worse, it survives as *convention,* partly because its outward forms offer some comfort in times of dislocation and partly because they continue to bind us to generations long gone. Tradition is an expression of faith; convention is what remains, because of its indisputable social usefulness, after faith has become problematical. Convention is exceedingly important because it is the mortar that holds together the bricks from which the edifice of society is made—to such a great degree, indeed, does the secular remain indebted to an unacknowledged sacred that it cannot quite dismiss. So patience remains one of our conventional secular values. How could it be otherwise?

We learn in our families and through our games that we must be patient. How can the acquisition of skills and the practice to maintain them be sustained where patience is lacking? How can we learn to take turns if there are no curbs on the disorderly potential of impatience? How could husband and wife or parent and child live in mutuality and trust where patience does not afford time and opportunity for forgiveness and reconciliation? How can one learn to risk and dare and dream, if there has been no patience within the family to establish a realm of basic trust where a child can afford to make mistakes without facing ridicule or harm? How shall we deal with the aged, the frail and infirm whose agility and memory have terribly declined, if we have not cultivated the habits of patience and caring?

Eventually a child must exercise what has been learned in the family and at play in a social world where cooperation and competition constantly demand perseverance and forbearance and the patient endurance of neglect, indifference, and delay. Patience is a civic virtue. Without civility and tolerance and courtesy the functioning of society will be so greatly impeded that it will no longer prosper. Law and respect for law are not sufficient social bonds; much more is essential in order to assure that people will feel comfortable with and not threatened by the presence of others. In our larger affairs, there can be no representative government without the patience that sustains an electoral process, no free enterprise system without the patience that encourages entrepreneurship, very little scientific progress or artistic creativity without the patience that supports the vitality of the imagination. Common sense hastens to the defense of convention: in many forms and many ways, patience is a civic virtue that we simply cannot do without. All this we know, or believe we know, but such knowledge will not suffice.

As the relationship between convention and tradition grows obscure and is deemed of little importance, the power of convention to shape human affairs is gradually eroded, despite all its reinforcement by common sense. So rudeness and dismissiveness become the order of the day. Words and ideas that have lost their specific religious reference and force are infiltrated by new assumptions that are inimical to the old. Therefore we confront two problems for which there are no easy solutions. The first is that conventions are never quite regarded as authoritative. They have no answer to give us when we ask what is wrong with unconventionality—simple indifference toward the conventions that dominate the lives of other people unless they serve our own purposes. So conventions are ultimately defenseless in the light of changed cultural assumptions.

For example, the assumption that immediate gratification is the birthright of an affluent society, where advertising instills cravings we otherwise could not even imagine, suggests that all waiting is deprivation. Changed cultural assumptions also affect the whole gamut of politics, economics, and communication, where the horizon is the next quarter, never the next year. The media focus on war and starvation in one country today, in another tomorrow, and never look back, reinforcing our suspicion that everything is episodic and there is no narrative quality to life where patience might be a virtue still, even a medium of revelation. Impatience flourishes with especial vigor whenever we encounter frustration and delay. Why wait? What is money for if it will not buy us preferential treatment, purchase the time and space that really belong to others but which we covet and can so easily afford? Why value perseverance in a world that promises instant gratification? Why prize endurance if we live in a world without consequences? Why is waiting a virtue if today's results are the only ones that matter, while longer perspectives are derided and go without reward?

Another problem is that the conventional meanings of ideas themselves slip and slide, eventually coming to express new assumptions. Sometimes they even fall into strange reversals of themselves, so that their meanings today plainly contradict much of what they conveyed in earlier times. Ironically, to insist on the importance of a convention in its contemporary form can distance us even further from what it originally described. That is why we should not call for the recovery of the virtue of patience until we are certain that we know what it means. Does patience have to do with passivity or action, vulnerability or strength, disciplining the passions or abolishing them, indifference to externals or concern for others? It can mean either the one or the other or both.

When others tell us to be patient, for example, all too often they mean we should be careful what impressions we give to other people. What is really important is the way that others perceive us, not our own feelings. The focus lies upon appearances, not reality, upon the reactions of others, not our own tendencies to anger and distraction or the need to develop self-restraint. The invocation of patience advises us to disguise our feelings but says nothing about disciplining and taming what we feel, so that we might become more fully the masters of our circumstances. This version of patience is sterile, of course. It contributes nothing to the growth of the self. In contrast, both in classical literature and throughout the Christian tradition there are countless admonitions that a cheerful countenance avails not at all if it masks an unquiet and resentful heart. So it seems clear that modern versions of old virtues sometimes bear no particular relation to the religious tradition from which they once drew their power and ultimate legitimacy. When patience is confused with permissiveness, indulgence, leniency, or resignation, it simply reveals how far from its original meanings the idea has come.

If patience is no longer something we aspire to, except for the sake of appearances, we nonetheless continue to urge others to be patient. We tell children and the aged who are no longer able to care for themselves to sit still, keep quiet, and be patient—because we have lost our patience with them. When we tell our children to be patient, moreover, are we not acknowledging that we ourselves are vulnerable to annoyance and vexation, and not really very patient at all? What we are asking for is not patience but silence, no matter how unwilling and sullen and angry. Here patience is wholly identified with passivity and submission. It is what the world's victims ask of those who might in some small fashion relieve their burdens. The invocation of patience is a sign that warns, "Do not disturb." Out of sight, out of mind—and so what need for further patience now? That is how a language can

gradually become a foreign tongue, no longer a reliable carrier of the freight of meaning it once so precisely and richly conveyed.

The following chapters sketch the important history, the impoverished present, and the urgent future of the idea of patience in the Christian tradition. Patience once described an essential aspect of moral selfhood, regardless of the presence or absence of any religious commitment, and identified conventions such as civility and courtesy that are simple necessities of life together. What is most important from a Christian perspective, however, is that patience also designates one of God's own principal perfections. It summarizes the redemptive obedience of the Suffering Servant, and denotes a theological virtue so important that without it there can be no Christian life at all. It is such an extraordinarily rich and complex idea in its array of meanings, in its usage in the biblical narrative, and in its later history that it invites sustained exploration in both theology and ethics.

The figures from the history of the church discussed in these pages form a diverse group; they represent different traditions and different ages and they certainly do not speak with a single voice. Nor do they include all of the most influential and innovative writers on patience. A comprehensive list would surely include not only Lactantius, John Cassian, Peter Damian, Catherine of Siena, Jeremias Drexel, and Francis de Sales, but a great parade of others.[10] The themes of a particular author are not necessarily unique—they would be much less important if they were—nor do they consistently dominate all the other refrains in his text. In every case, however, they are characteristic emphases that are phrased in distinctive ways

and that exercised considerable influence upon the further development of the Christian tradition. These are representative writers: they built on what they inherited and bequeathed still more on which those who came after them could build. They furnish some of the threads in a great tapestry, the design of which has a subtlety and a complexity that could not be encompassed by the eyes of one individual alone.

We have said that the significance of patience has become elusive and obscure for much contemporary Christian reflection. Is it simply a minor virtue, one among many, or is it, as some of these authors have alleged, the "highest" or the "chief" or the "root of all" virtue? This essay certainly does not advance the claim that patience is first or foremost among the virtues, except in the sense that without it there can be no Christian virtue at all. But if patience, and humility as well, are dismissed as minor virtues, we are the ones who will be impoverished, adrift from moorings in rivers of our own tradition.

The issue is very simple. If life is dialogue, mutuality, and responsiveness, then patience is at its center. If life is domination of dependents and subordinates, of all who are weaker or poorer, then patience is nonsense—except, of course, for the losers in the war of all against all. Perhaps impatience is not the original human sin—though some would argue that it is—but there has been consistent agreement within the Christian tradition that impatience does not signify merely the absence of a single virtue but the erosion of them all. It is not one fault among the many perils that confront us; it renders the self vulnerable to the whole spectrum of vices, each and every one. The notions of patience and humility are not anachronisms in the modern world. Those words are part of a vocabulary of virtue hallowed by two millennia of Christian usage and yet sometimes still as fresh as when it first was minted, quite unsurpassed for raising the question, What must we acquire if we are to find a rewarding and enjoyable life? Patience is much of the answer. If our future should involve a certain erosion

of independence, as technology renders us in some ways dependent on our social environment, the importance and dignity of patience will become all the more apparent.

Chapter Two

The Patience of God

the Hebrew and Christian scriptures

Toward the end of the Old Testament, its most humorous book presents us with the story of an impatient man who wishes for an impatient god and never quite understands that he owes his life to the God who exercised patient forbearance toward him when he did not deserve it. When God calls Jonah to serve as his prophet in the great city of Nineveh and tells him, "Go and cry out against it" (1:2), Jonah flees to Joppa and boards the first ship bound for Tarshish—no Nineveh for him. But God's patience is eventually rewarded when, after suffering the terrors of a violent storm and being swallowed by a huge fish, Jonah begs for deliverance. God speaks to the fish, which disgorges Jonah on a beach, and then the reluctant prophet turns his feet toward Nineveh, a place of much wickedness.

His message is that the city will be overthrown in forty days because of the evil ways of its inhabitants. The people heed Jonah's preaching, however; they repent in sackcloth and ashes, and declare a fast in the hope that God will forbear and

avert his anger from them. And, "when God saw what they did, how they turned from their evil ways, God changed his mind about the calamity that he had said he would bring upon them; and he did not do it" (3:10). This leaves Jonah not merely disconsolate but furious. Divine forbearance not only deprives him of all the pleasure of serving God in Nineveh—he went there, of course, for the promised spectacle of retribution—but to his own mind justifies his original decision to flee to Tarshish. Is it not folly to count on a God such as this to exact retribution promptly, richly, and with full dramatic effect?

With wonderful irony Jonah, forgetful that he himself still lives only because of the patience that God continued to exercise, accuses God of—patience! He recites Israel's confession of faith as an accusation against a Lord who fails to display impatience and vengeance in response to human sin:

> Is not this what I said while I was still in my own country? That is why I fled to Tarshish at the beginning; for I knew that you are a gracious God and merciful, slow to anger, and abounding in steadfast love, and ready to relent from punishing. (Jonah 4:2)

A God gracious and merciful, slow to anger and ready to relent—in a word, patient—is scarcely what one hopes to find at the end of a search for an angry and impatient judge in heaven, and so Jonah goes away sorrowing. We do not know what happens to him. What we do know is that Jonah, utterly despite himself and yet without any infringement on his own freedom, has become part of a new beginning that conserves and extends the old beginnings in Adam, Cain, Noah, Abraham, and the rest, because the Patient One of Israel has not finished with his creatures yet.

Time and again the Bible declares that God is gracious, merciful, and patient. At Sinai the LORD says to Moses, "The

LORD, the LORD, a God merciful and gracious, slow to anger, and abounding in steadfast love and faithfulness" (Exodus 34:6). The same triad appears with small variations in a number of other places, especially in the psalms. Whatever else one might sometimes wish to say of God, one is always speaking of the Lord whose patience extends from everlasting to everlasting. If we ascribe impatience to God, we would be speaking not of God but of an idol of our own devising. One scholar, speaking of God's "steady persistence," aptly comments: "The most important of all the distinctive ideas of the Old Testament is God's steady and extraordinary persistence in continuing to love wayward Israel in spite of Israel's insistent waywardness."[1] When we search the scriptures for references to patience or for assurances that the patience of God is unfailing, however, we find that not one verse in the King James Version, for centuries the most influential translation of the Bible into English, contains the word "patience" until we reach the gospels. But there are many other words that express at least a part of its meaning—such as forbearance, perseverance, and persistence, endurance, long-suffering, and slowness to anger, faithfulness and constancy—because the idea itself is so central to the whole narrative of scripture. The patience of God is the very heart of the story.

The Bible begins with the great affirmation that God is Creator. When God offers the gift of life to Adam and Eve, he gives them time and space of their own, a realm for the free expression of their liberty. He does not crowd the people he has made in any way at all. Instead, he creates for them a garden in which to exercise their own initiative and inventiveness, and offers them dominion over everything within it. God is not grudging with his gifts, but patiently awaits the fruits of the stewardship he has granted them. When Adam and Eve

impatiently reject the freedom God has generously given them in favor of the illusory and sterile liberty of the serpent, they become the slaves of the creation they were intended to rule. In his patience, however, "the LORD God made garments of skins for the man and his wife, and clothed them" (Genesis 3:21) in order to protect them in what has now become an alien world, before they are sent into exile to endure the punishment they have brought upon themselves.

Patience is not essential to creativity. The potter can always smash a pot to shards and begin anew. But this Creator never does so; he discloses himself in creation and redemption as a God whose patience endures from everlasting to everlasting. Each of his new beginnings renews and reaffirms the beginnings that preceded it; every judgment is redemptive and proclaims that he will not cast off forever the ones whom he has judged. Every punishment implies that he has not yet revoked the promises given to the creatures he has made. While God may appear to turn his back upon humanity for a season, there is never room for doubt: he has not finished with us yet. The disclosure of divine patience and forbearance in the saga of creation is repeated in each of the narratives that follows the tale of the disobedience of Adam and Eve.

The second story is the account of Abel and Cain, who is both the inheritor of evil and himself bent upon it, compounding with murder his parents' impatient rebelliousness. When Cain exclaims that his punishment for slaying his brother is greater than he can bear because now he is not only cursed by God but is himself liable to become a victim of murder, the LORD places his mark upon Cain and says, "Not so! Whoever kills Cain will suffer a sevenfold vengeance" (Genesis 4:15). The focus really lies not upon Cain but on the patience of God, who decrees that the murderer shall not be punished by the death he deserves. Instead, there shall be a

fresh beginning through Cain's son Enoch, who would not have been conceived had it not been for God's patient forbearance.

In the third tale, at the center of the stage there is not a lone malefactor but the one righteous individual who remains in the midst of an otherwise utterly corrupt and wicked generation. Although God determines "to make an end of all flesh, for the earth is filled with violence because of them" (Genesis 6:13), his patience again reveals itself in preserving Noah and his family and establishing a covenant with them and their descendants forever. The LORD will not again send a flood to destroy the earth. God blesses Noah and commands him to be fruitful, to multiply and fill the earth. This new beginning reaffirms and extends the first beginning in Eden, for the gracious words of permission are unmistakably reminiscent of the words God uttered in the garden. A rainbow will be the sign of the covenant with Noah. This promise written on the clouds is somehow a reminder of the mark with which Cain is branded—that token of his fratricide but also a sign of God's protection.

In the tale of the tower of Babel, where creatures directly assault the Creator's sovereignty, the emphasis shifts from individuals who are either wicked or righteous to the iniquity and faithlessness that infect the entire human community and from which no one is exempt. The story portrays the radical outcome of Adam's fall, from the isolated crime of his own son Cain to the collective sin among the artisans of the tower, from the assault upon the life of a single fellow creature to the attack upon the divine source of all life.

> So the LORD scattered them abroad from there over the face of all the earth, and they left off building the city. Therefore it was called Babel, because there the LORD confused the language of all the earth. (Genesis 11:8-9)

But if the LORD deprives them of their homes and common language, he does not annul the gift of life. In merely scattering them abroad, he displays still more richly his patience and forbearance.

But now there is no covenantal sign as there was in the two previous stories; patience is not accompanied by any renewal of the divine promise. The answer, of course, is that all else is prologue to the climactic event that follows the tale of Babel, the calling of Abraham and the renewal of the covenant once for all. Karl Barth, who alone among the major theologians of the twentieth century has written extensively of God's patience, asks:

> Does not the grace and mercy of God depend upon the fact that there is also a patience of God, that He grants space to the sinful creature, thus giving Himself space further to speak and act with it?...Since He has willed to provide us with the sign of Cain and that of Noah, do we not have to say that the omnipotent Godhead of the living God consists only in the fact that He is not impatient but patient?[2]

Instead of annulling the life of him who out of impatience first destroys life, God's patience declares that Cain not only will be preserved against his enemies but will be the parent of the heirs to the divine patience enshrined in the covenant with Noah and in the promises to Abraham. All nations will be blessed by the extension of the patience shown to the first murderer. To a new generation descended from the people he scattered from the tower of Babel God promises a land flowing with milk and honey, which in the context of the covenant renews the original gift to Adam and Eve of unbegrudged time and space.

Creation and covenant, the two great themes to which the Old Testament introduces us, are complementary meditations on the patience of God. God offers the gift of life, and not only

life but room, time and space that provide his creatures with opportunities for the exercise of responsibility and creativeness and for the expression of gratitude and joy. Into all this room for the inventiveness of finite freedom God comes again and again in order to show forbearance and offer deliverance so that human liberty can be restored when his creatures have thrown it away. Like the covenants, creation is grace. The sins that these four stories rehearse are crimes of ever-increasing magnitude: from impatient disobedience to fratricide to universal iniquity to the arrogant attempt to displace God himself. What is so thoroughly remarkable in the biblical narrative is that each escalation of human sinfulness is met by a still greater display of divine patience. First there is the simple gift of clothes so that Adam and Eve need not go naked into exile, then the protection offered to Cain, later the everlasting covenant established with Noah and, in the end, the great promise made to Abraham and his children. Creaturely rebellion always becomes an occasion for new revelations of an unchallengeable strength of patience that nothing whatsoever can deter. Patience is not in tension with omnipotence but is, in fact, the vehicle for its progressive expression.

Whether God comes to comfort or judge, renew or punish, the essential message is always the same: I have not finished with you yet. It is a fearsome thing; indeed, to encounter the patience of the living God. It is wrong, therefore, to interpret divine patience as one might treat his wrath, as though it were an attitude that is sometimes displayed in God's transactions with the world and sometimes not. There is no warrant in the Old Testament for the assumption that divine patience can be so taxed and even exhausted that eventually it must yield to something else altogether, and then human apostasy and injustice will reap the retribution they so richly deserve. On the contrary: everything else is an expression of God's patience, even though the eyes of the sinner cannot always discern the ways that it undergirds and inspires the whole range of divine operations. The lapse of patience would mean the total revocation of time and space, the annulling of the creature, the swallowing of all light by everlasting darkness—though God would remain forever, rich and complete and undiminished in himself.

The early stories of the Genesis narrative point toward the fulfillment of the great eschatological visions of the prophets, when the invincible power of God's patience will sweep away all else before it. Isaiah's prophecy of the Prince of Peace, Deutero-Isaiah's foretelling of the Suffering Servant, Jeremiah's vision of the new covenant, and Ezekiel's tidings of the Good Shepherd tell of the sovereign freedom of God to exercise patience in order to overcome all sin, heal all brokenness, and restore the world in accordance with God's design. Isaiah portrays the Suffering Servant as one who bore "our transgressions," was "crushed for our iniquities," because "the LORD has laid on him the iniquity of us all" (Isaiah 53:5-6). His endurance displayed such patience that "he did not open his mouth; like a lamb that is led to the slaughter, and like a sheep before his shearers is silent" (Isaiah 53:7). Here is the human and more than human paradigm of patience in the Old Testament: one who finds fulfillment through suffering, whose obedient perseverance is action undertaken in behalf of all those in bondage, whose steadfast endurance is triumphantly redemptive not only for Israel but for all the nations that through Israel will be blessed.

The faithful and uncomplaining endurance of the servant points toward another fundamental meaning of patience—

expectant waiting that puts anxiety to flight. Such waiting is profoundly different from mere submission; instead, it is always filled with anticipation and confidence, with the faith that in a world where God rules someone or something will appear that will help or comfort or alter the situation. So waiting patiently is suffused with a certain joy on the one hand, because the certainty of God's patience means there are possibilities and opportunities as yet unexplored, and with a certain humility on the other, because the self cannot trust in its own strength but must await resources other than its own. Despite all the unknowns and uncertainties that waiting entails, however, there is nonetheless peace and joy.

The unvarying message of the prophets has a stark simplicity. The Holy One of Israel is gracious, merciful, and long-suffering; he has elected this people, given to them and preserved for them time and space so they might be a blessing to all nations. But they have misunderstood their election, seeing it as privilege rather than responsibility, refusing to imitate the righteousness and patience of God in their dealings with others or among themselves. They have fallen into injustice and pride. So they are called to repent. God in his patience wills to be merciful. If they do not return to him, however, terrible punishment will ensue, precisely because God will never simply turn his back on those whom he has chosen. Thus judgment is not an end in itself but the prelude to a new beginning that will renew and reaffirm all the beginnings that preceded it. God's freedom does not threaten but establishes the freedom of the creature. His power does not annihilate but conserves the powers of what he has made, for patience is its characteristic mode of expression. Of this patience Karl Barth writes:

> We define God's patience as His will, deep-rooted in His essence and constituting his divine being and action, to

> allow to another—for the sake of His own grace and mercy and in the affirmation of his holiness and justice—space and time for the development of its own existence, thus conceding to this existence a reality side by side with His own.[3]

The Old Testament does not boast of the faithfulness of a great people and their indomitable patience despite all the afflictions they must bear. On the contrary, the Hebrew scriptures recount the faithfulness and patience of God toward an impatient and faithless tribe. This is perhaps what distinguishes them most profoundly from every other of the world's sacred texts.

Patience is at the center of the New Testament as well, although it has distinctive accents because of its references to Jesus Christ, to the mission of the church, and to the imminence of the Second Coming. But no matter how rich and various its meanings, the basic forms of the virtue are not difficult to describe.

First, patience signifies forbearance, which does not mean permissiveness or indulgence but the gift of room, time and space for the amendment of life. The author of the first letter to Timothy tells us that "Christ Jesus came into the world to save sinners—of whom I am the foremost. But for that very reason I received mercy, so that in me, as the foremost, Jesus Christ might display the utmost patience" (1:15-16). God's forbearance finds its climactic expression in the inexhaustible patience of him who is the model for all those within the Christian community.

Second, patience is the persistence revealed in all God's dealings with his creatures from the first Adam to the last, and

shown forth in the obedience of Jesus Christ. Third is the calm and uncomplaining endurance of pain and adversity, suffering for righteousness' sake, where again Christ is the paradigm. It is important to note that there is a double-sidedness to this endurance. He endures all that his enemies inflict upon him because he is perfectly responsive to his Father's will. Endurance entails responsiveness as well as bearing pain: Jesus suffers the initiative of God, in the sense that his will is wholly subordinated to the will of the Father. Were this not true, his physical suffering would be devoid of redemptive significance. So Christian faith has traditionally spoken of both the active and the passive obedience of the Son, who is obedient first to God and then to his tormentors.

Finally, there is waiting with equanimity and expectancy, because he who has come is coming again:

> Be patient, therefore, beloved, until the coming of the Lord. The farmer waits for the precious crop from the earth, being patient with it until it receives the early and the late rains. You also must be patient. Strengthen your hearts, for the coming of the Lord is near. (James 5:7-8)

For faith there is already the sense of an ending that illuminates the unfinished narratives of the present and invests this time between the times with joyful anticipation. This eschatological note is repeated in some of the parables of Jesus, including the story of the barren fig tree which its owner decides to cast away until the gardener pleads that it be preserved for another year (Luke 13:6-9). Perhaps patience will have its reward, perhaps not, but what hope could there be if patience were not shown? The heart of the little story is the forbearance of the owner of the vineyard, who continues to exercise patience toward even the least promising of all his holdings.

Another parable tells of a servant who is forgiven a great debt when he pleads with his master for patience, but who then demonstrates no forbearance toward a fellow servant who owes him a small amount, casting him into prison instead. When the lord hears what his servant has done, he sends him to prison as well, asking, "Should you not have had mercy on your fellow slave, as I had mercy on you?" (Matthew 18:33). Part of the moral is that one should not judge lest one is judged oneself and found waiting. God alone is judge and if he patiently withholds his judgment, who are we to claim for ourselves his prerogative? Patient forbearance is one key without which the gates of the kingdom will remain forever locked.

Perhaps the most familiar of the parables is the story of the prodigal son, who leaves his family and travels to a far country where he squanders all his patrimony in riotous living. After poverty and hunger lead him to envy a herd of swine the food that he has been hired to throw to them, he repents and returns to his father, declaring that he is now unworthy to be treated as more than a hired servant (Luke 15:11-32). But his father embraces him and prepares a lavish feast in his honor. When another son who has remained unswervingly obedient to his parent remonstrates, the father responds: "This brother of yours was dead and has come to life; he was lost and has been found" (v. 32).

Like the parables of the lost sheep and the lost coin that immediately precede it, the story of the prodigal son tells of the joy at finding what was lost. The focus is primarily on the father, not on either of the sons. Without the exercise of patience, what hope could there ever be for reconciliation, for the healing and restoration of relationships, for a shared future? How can the lost ever be found if patience does not enable light to strike the heart of the darkness where coins and sheep are hidden? Although the prodigal son and his father could never have been

reunited except for the boy's repentance, the emphasis lies not on this but on the father's forbearance, the persistence of his love, his patient waiting when there seemed no reason to wait, his reluctance to sit in judgment, his readiness to put behind himself all righteous indignation despite everything.

Another Lucan parable is the story of the sower, some of whose seed is scattered upon a pathway, some on rocks, some among thorns, and some on fertile ground (Luke 8:5-8). The soil trodden by many feet or strewn with rocks or filled with thorns represents different sorts of persons who hear but do not heed the gospel; they are graced neither with the strength to endure adversity, nor with the capacity to persevere, nor with the ability to wait calmly and not succumb to worldly diversions. In contrast to all these who seem to be the victims of impatience in one form or another, there are the ones who furnish good soil because they believe and stand firm, who "when they hear the word, hold it fast in an honest and good heart, and bear fruit with patient endurance" (8:15). It is by patience that the kingdom is won. The eschatological emphasis of all these parables reinforces the urgency of imitating the patience of him who is coming soon but who patiently defers the day of judgment so that the church might fulfill its mission to proclaim the gospel to all people.

The Sermon on the Mount in Matthew's gospel is a rich and complex text of many parts, and it is extraordinary how much of it can be read as a gloss on the meaning of patience. Most of the beatitudes are concerned with those who are patient—the poor in spirit or humble ones who wait patiently for God's help, the mourners who patiently bear their afflictions without complaint, the meek who patiently practice forbearance, the merciful who patiently disavow the idea of vengeance, the peacemakers whose patience creates tranquility where there has been discord, and those who patiently endure persecution

and evil for Christ's sake. Thereafter, the lengthy pericopes on murder and the *lex talionis*—an eye for an eye and a tooth for a tooth—both relativize dictates of the law in accordance with the counsels of true patience.

The core of the hymn to Christian love in 1 Corinthians 13 lies in verses four to eight, which characterize love in eight ways. These are juxtaposed to eight acts or attitudes that are arrayed against it. Its first affirmation is that love is patient; the seven attributes that follow can all be read as standing in apposition to "patient" and as clarifications of its meaning. Love is kind and rejoices when others have the time and space in which to flourish, never begrudging them a sufficiency of room of their own. It bears, believes, hopes, and endures all things, and it never ends—forbearing because this is an essential dimension of bearing all things without thirsting for the retribution that patience knows must be left to God alone.

Not all love of humans for one another is patient, however. Persons can do great harm to each other by the excesses of their loving, while impatience has the capacity to transform someone beloved into an object of hate. Nor is all human patience loving; it can be ruthless and implacable in its thralldom to envy or lust or revenge or greed. But Christian love is a gift of grace and an imitation of the love disclosed in Jesus Christ. Therefore, just as Christian patience is rooted in love, so also does Christian love always display the patience that finds its perfect realization in the obedience of the Son. In the three words of 1 Corinthians—"love is patient"—we have a matchless summary of much of the whole narrative of scripture.

In writing to the church at Rome, Paul contrasts Adam and Christ: "Just as by the one man's disobedience the many were made sinners, so by the one man's obedience the many will be made righteous" (Romans 5:19). The great passage in the second chapter of Philippians explains this obedience more

expansively and offers its own special testimony to the centrality of patience for the Christian life. Paul exhorts the congregation at Philippi to put on the mind of Christ, who emptied and humbled himself and made himself nothing (Philippians 2:5-8). He *emptied* and *humbled* himself: how can we approach the meaning of these two verbs? The early Christian creeds, with stark and simple economy, use a single word to comprehend the whole of the way of the Christ, his ministry and teaching and passion and obedience unto death: they tell us that he "suffered." How can such an ordinary word convey Christ's reconciling work?

Part of the answer, as we have seen, is that suffering must be distinguished from the experience of pain or the feeling of sorrow. It can entail one or the other but often it involves neither, as when we "suffer" the solicitude of a friend or the attention and care of a parent or teacher. So suffering is reason for gratitude as well as for sadness; it suggests the enrichment of life as much as its diminution. Suffering represents the way our opportunities and attitudes are shaped for better and for worse by the words and deeds of other people, whose initiatives are so often necessary if we are to find our own. Responsible life is attentive suffering, because only by way of it are we truly set free. Irresponsible life is inattentive suffering. The universality of suffering, therefore, is not merely an accidental truth of the human situation but its essence. It is our inescapable condition; it is how we enter and leave our world.

We have said that life is made up of encounters and meetings, mutuality and dialogue. So its fundamental unit is "you and I" and never the self alone. We are made for communion: Eve is called into existence because "it is not good that the man should be alone" (Genesis 2:18). The root meaning of patience is suffering. To be a person is to be a patient, both in society and before God. In part, patience is such

a central theme in the Bible because it is implied in the scriptural notion of life as dialogue with other creatures and the Creator. Faith is the patient attempt to realize our possibilities as *patients* before God, while unbelief is the impatient denial that the condition of patient can lead to fulfillment and the vain attempt to seize the initiative that belongs only to God. Unbelief leads to boredom, loneliness, and the destruction of the self.

The paradigm of patience in the New Testament is the *kenosis*, self-emptying, of Christ. Jesus is the second Adam, a human being as well as the disclosure of what humanity was created to be. Like all people, therefore, he suffers—but he does not suffer as we do. Like all people, he is a patient—but in Jesus alone there is no impatience at all. His perfect patience reveals the invincibility of the patience of the Father against every obstacle, and there are unique dimensions to his patience in each of the four forms his suffering takes. First, Jesus suffers at the hands of others—not only his enemies, but so many others who have ears but do not hear, so many who have eyes but do not see. As he approaches the cross, Jesus is increasingly solitary and his suffering is exacerbated by the severance of each earthly tie until not one of them remains. He is patient until every single thing has been taken away.

Second, Jesus suffers the assaults of the powers of darkness, who recognize that he is the Son of God. As an exorcist, Jesus is engaged with demons in a struggle that has mysterious cosmic aspects. Third, he suffers the wrath of God, submitting without complaint to the inescapable destiny of the sinner. For our sake he stands in our place and accepts the judgment that falls upon the whole human race. He bears it entirely away, but the cost is utter loneliness beneath the divine "No." Isolated and without kin in his separation from the source of life, he is bereft of all companionship.

Finally, Jesus suffers in the sense that he is wholly responsive to the Father's initiative, and this is the meaning of the words "he emptied himself...he humbled himself." In the end, nothing whatsoever is withheld: the self is emptied of everything until it becomes a pure transparency to the will of God, who sent him. It is this particular mode of suffering, his "active" obedience, which invests all his other "passive" sufferings with their redemptive significance. It is his utterly selfless patience that points beyond itself to the mercy of God the Father. This is not the absence of initiative, but its perfection: only he who possesses himself fully can yield himself fully, and only he who is one with the Father possesses the self in such fashion that he is able to offer it whole and without reservation. It is precisely in his willingness to suffer even abandonment at the hands of God, in his totally unreserved passibility before the Holy One, in his patient endurance before God's irrevocable negation, that Jesus discloses his oneness with the Father. In the final earthly helplessness of the Son we see the power of the Father's patience and caring.

"Jesus Christ is the meaning of God's patience," writes Barth.[4] The cross of Christ testifies to divine patience that can be contested by no other power, but never trespasses upon creaturely freedom. It is a divine perfection, the inmost nature of a Creator who never begrudges time or space or liberty to what he has made—not even to fallen Adam or accursed Cain, or the architects of Babel or impatient Jonah. If we wish to speak of God from a Christian perspective, we must speak of God's patience. Christians are called to imitate the patience of the Father and to participate in the patience of the Son, so that one can echo Paul's grateful words, "I yet not I but Christ in me." This paradox of grace is perhaps the finest expression of the nature of Christian patience as the selfless suffering of the initiative of God. In the end, patience is not only one dimension

of the obedience of Jesus Christ but so fundamental that this part can very well represent the whole. Patience is possibly as good a summary as we shall find of the life celebrated by the church's confession, "He suffered under Pontius Pilate." This is the secret of his redemptive work and the first of the great themes that must figure prominently in a constructive account of the virtue. Suffering is the destiny of us all. We must welcome and embrace many of its forms, for this is the road, the only road, to the potential our humanity enshrines.

Chapter Three

The Gift of Perseverance

Tertullian, Cyprian, and Augustine

Writing in Latin-speaking Africa in the middle of the third century, Cyprian of Carthage spoke with great beauty and persuasiveness of his conviction that patience lies at the heart of Christian discipleship. "The Word of God, silent, is led to the cross," Cyprian wrote. "He does not speak, nor is he moved, nor does he proclaim his majesty. . . . He endures all things even to the end, with constant perseverance, so that in Christ a full and perfect patience may find its realization."[1]

In the previous chapter we saw that although patience is an insistent refrain in the Bible, it is exemplified not by the chosen people, whose vocation it is to wait upon their Lord, but by the Lord who chooses to wait upon a rebellious people. Patience is one of the principal perfections of God, who endures betrayal with constant forbearance and awaits the repentance of those who flee from his persistent love. God is patient toward us

because he is patient in himself. It is in Jesus Christ that God's patience is fully expressed, for he accepts the status of patient and object among the creatures he has made. God himself is vulnerable; his capacity to suffer is the ultimate paradox of his power. Thus patience is perhaps the best of all synonyms for the way of the Christ.

The theologians of the early church appreciated the centrality of patience in the scriptures, although their emphases were sometimes rather different because of the reality of persecution and the expectation of the imminent end of world history. Theologians such as Tertullian and Cyprian of Carthage, and Augustine of Hippo, were also influenced by the Stoic tradition, which proved in some ways to be a useful instrument for the proclamation of the gospel. As Christianity pursued its mission to the gentile world, the need for a vocabulary intelligible outside the Jewish community was met from many sources, with Stoicism among the most important. The Stoic ideal of wisdom, as expressed in the writings of philosophers like Seneca, Epictetus, Cicero, and Marcus Aurelius, seemed to be a massive reinforcement of the nature of Christian discipleship and of the role of patience in its achievement.

Stoicism is the tradition in the West that has most eloquently insisted upon the preeminence among virtues of patience in one particular form. Eclectic and resolutely practical, it expressed the unsatisfied religious yearnings of late classical antiquity and provided an answer to those yearnings that was as attractive as it was difficult to attain—the sage as the perfect embodiment of patience. The passionlessness of the wise, so the Stoic philosophers believed, elevates them beyond all the worldly distractions that inhibit self-fulfillment and place happiness at risk. The wise are forever freed from the turbulence of the appetites that lacerate the foolish. In Seneca's words, the self is made the equal of God. The difference between the foolish and the wise is that the wise person knows it is folly to seek fulfillment in things that no one can control—such as the pursuit of ephemeral goods like wealth or fame or affection or power. Virtue and happiness have to do with an attitude of detachment, or else we become hostages to fortune. The wise know that happiness depends upon themselves alone.

The problem for the sage, therefore, is not the task of moderating and regulating the passions, discerning within them a mean between extremes. Instead, it is the challenge to extinguish their fires entirely, so that nothing remains to disturb the peace that true wisdom brings. The sage who has perfected self-mastery is someone who has achieved *apatheia*, apathy or passionlessness, which is the proper meaning of patience for Stoicism. This is the highest wisdom we can attain; it is what salvation signifies. Apathy (from *apathe*, without feeling) certainly does not mean ignorant and callous indifference, but rather release from every passion that might divert the self from its focus upon God. Writing of the endless turmoil that anger fosters, the philosopher Seneca asks, "Shall we not summon ourselves to patience when it promises so great a reward, the unmoved serenity of a happy mind?"[2]

But if the intellectual prominence of the Stoic tradition meant that Christian assessments of the value of patience for the life of faith did not seem entirely strange and alien, early Christian theologians also recognized its fundamental opposition to the gospel. While Stoicism sought to banish the passions, Christians valued them as gifts from God and sought to use them in God's service. Writing in the early fourth century, Lactantius explains that patience is inspired by "nothing other than fear of God." Therefore, "fear should not be torn away, as the Stoics wish, nor tempered, as the

Peripatetics hold, but it should be directed unto the true way... that all the rest are not feared." In what respect, he asks, "does a wise and good man differ from the foolish, unless it be because he possesses unconquered patience, which fools lack?"[3] For Lactantius, this is the greatest of all virtues. But surely pity and affection and generosity and loyalty also have their place, when they too are rooted in the fear of God.

Despite their shared view of the importance of patience, the contrasts between Christianity and Stoicism are more fundamental still. One speaks of ardor for God and the other of indifference toward God's world; one of faith and the other of reason; one of eschatological hope and the other of resignation. One tradition celebrates the love that inspires patience, and the other patience that has conquered love. One holds up self-sacrifice and the other self-sufficiency; one extols the love that is expressed in the midst of suffering, and the other sees suffering as the penalty for yielding to love. One stresses mercy encompassing the frail and ungodly, the other the enduring distinction between the wise and the foolish. One tradition speaks of submission to God and the other of equality. Small wonder, then, that the Christianization of the Stoic ideal proved as daunting as it was crucial if the church was to enlist its resources to proclaim the gospel to all sorts and conditions in the gentile world.

Perhaps the greatest danger of the early church's reliance on the Stoic ideal, however, was not that the notion of passionlessness could dull its appreciation of the importance of pity or compassion in human affairs. Instead, it was the possibility that uncritical and sometimes unconscious dependence upon Stoic definitions of patience—Lactantius' description of it as "enduring with equanimity the evils which are inflicted or fall upon one"[4] is an example—could distract the attention of the church from other aspects of patience that

were of central importance in the Bible but not part of this philosophical context. Certainly the biblical view of patience as God's forbearance could not fit comfortably within the scientific outlook of Stoicism, nor the insistent biblical refrain that patience is expectant waiting, filled with anticipations of what is to come.

Of the most important early Christian writings on patience, this chapter will concentrate on the theologians who lived and worked in Carthage and Hippo, the territory to the west of the city of Alexandria where Clement and Origen labored in the shadow of the greatest library of late antiquity. We will focus on three theologians who were not only the most widely respected Christian authors to emerge in Latin-speaking Africa, but also among the most important figures of the early church—Tertullian, Cyprian, and Augustine.

Who knows whether or not it was his education in Stoic philosophy that emboldened Tertullian, in the first important Christian treatise on patience, to argue that patience is "the highest virtue" because no one would claim to be wise without first domesticating the unruliness of the passions? But it was unquestionably Christian faith that undergirded Tertullian's high estimation of patience and furnished him with the distinctive emphases of his own interpretation. It was faith that led him to contrast so sharply the patience that has its source in God alone with the merely "human product" invented by pagan philosophers who do not acknowledge that patience is "the very nature of God," a perfection of the divine essence. Where God is, there is patience, the "child of his nurturing" and the "inseparable companion" of his Spirit.[5]

For Tertullian, patience can be rightly interpreted only in the light of God's revelation. On the one hand, there is the revelation from on high. God makes the sun to rise on the just and the unjust, preserving the world even when it has become a theater for the expression of ingratitude and sin, for through patience God hopes to draw them to himself. On the other hand, we have the revelation of this forbearance "within our reach" through the Incarnation. Every aspect of the life and teaching and passion of Jesus eloquently proclaims the inexhaustible patience of a Father who never falters in his quest for every lost sheep and prodigal child. "Marvel at the constancy of His meekness," Tertullian continues. "He who had proposed to escape notice in the guise of man has in no degree imitated man's impatience....Patience such as this no mere man had ever practiced." Indeed, the very magnitude of such patience is the stumbling block that causes pagans to reject the gospel. Patience is really a synonym for the whole obedience of the Redeemer—actually, Tertullian writes, obedience itself "stems from patience." It is the basis for reconciliation, for how could healing be either offered or accepted if God were to remain impatiently intent upon the redress of injury?[6]

As for the triad of great Christian virtues, faith is what "the patience of Christ has instilled," hope has to do with our own patient anticipation, and Christian love, which patience invariably accompanies, can hardly be learned "except by the exercise of patience." Patience is the fruit of each and all of them, just as they are each and all its progeny. In the life of discipleship, how can one ever determine which is first and which is last, or which is greatest and which is least? All are the gifts of God's grace. Tertullian speaks of another virtue, however, which is not often mentioned explicitly but is an implicit theme of his essay, binding together all its various parts. It first appears in Tertullian's confession that he is someone "of

no account" who dares to write of something he does not himself possess, and will someday attain only if God should condescend to grant it. That is the humility exemplified by the life of Christ, without which patience is no more than an impossible dream. Humility is the source and reason for patience, and patience is the test of true humility: without the one, there is no hope for the other. "Who is humble," he asks, "but the man who is patient?"[7]

There are some accents in Tertullian's essay that become familiar refrains in other writings on patience and are worth mentioning for that reason. One is his distinguishing between patience of the soul, or spirit, and the complementary patience of the flesh, or body, a distinction that Tertullian uses in order to present his own ascetical version of the gospel. Patience of the flesh means self-denial, which offers "a sacrifice of mourning dress along with meager rations, contenting itself with plain food and a drink of clear water, joining fast with fast and persevering in sackcloth and ashes."[8] Such ordinary instances of self-denial are crowned by vows of continence, by the physical torments of persecution and imprisonment, and above all by the patient courage of martyrs in the face of death. This notion of patience as asceticism is no less important than it is foreign to the meanings the virtue suggests today, but it would be remiss to omit it entirely from a constructive account of the virtue for contemporary life.

Tertullian also echoes the Stoic tradition in its high regard for self-control. He extols the stoic indifference that overcomes pain and enables the self to become the master of its passions. Finally, though it may seem extraordinary that someone trained in Roman jurisprudence should write of patience as the fulfillment of the law, Tertullian insists that the *lex talionis*, the punitive return of evil for evil, expresses nothing more than the reign of impatience in the lives of sinners. Compensation

involves the victim in the perpetrator's own unrighteousness, for there is no difference between them except that "the one is caught doing wrong sooner than the other." Patience has no recourse to the courts, heeds the admonition not to judge lest one be judged oneself, and acknowledges no pain. Therefore, because the victim's silent endurance of pain deprives the evildoer of any satisfaction, "he will himself inevitably feel pain because he has lost his reward." Patience fulfills the law because it stifles the thirst for revenge, establishes an eschatological perspective that eases the burdens of the present age, and humbly recognizes that judgment must be exercised by the Lord alone. For the Christian, "not even a lawful injury is permitted."[9]

What is least expected and most important in the whole essay, however, is Tertullian's treatment of impatience. More than anything else, he tells us, impatience is "opposed to faith." The origin of impatience lies with the devil himself. Tertullian argues it does not matter whether the devil was originally evil or simply impatient: "It is clear that, whether impatience had its beginning in evil or evil in impatience, they entered into combination and grew as one in the bosom of one father." Impatience with the divine decision to grant dominion over all the world to a creature made in God's own image impelled Satan to tempt the woman to transgress the divine command. Impatience led Eve to sin and impatience persuaded Adam to join in her disobedience. For Tertullian, therefore, impatience is our original sin. It is an ingredient in every other sin whatsoever, no matter how different they might at first appear. His example is Cain's murder of Abel. Since impatience

> had plunged Adam and Eve into death, it taught their son, also, to commit the first murder.... Such was the cradle of impatience which was then... in its infancy. But to what

> proportions it soon grew! And no wonder: if it was the prime source of sin, it follows that, being the prime source, it was therefore also the sole fashioner of all sin, pouring forth from its own abundant resources the varied channels of crimes.

Therefore, Tertullian concludes, "every sin is to be traced back to impatience."[10]

If impatience is the work of the devil, our first parents' original sin and the source and inspiration of every transgression since, then patience is surely the key to the kingdom of God. It is all the more so because this gift of grace, as Tertullian views it, is at the center of obedience, discipleship, and faith. Here is a second major theme that must shape a constructive account of the virtue of patience: the endlessly destructive consequences of impatience. Few lessons could be more relevant for an age as impatient as our own.

Tertullian ends by reminding his readers that the devil sows his own sort of patience, oriented toward acquisition of the goods of this world and toward vengeance against all who stand in the way. The offspring of greed and envy and pride, patience of this kind is really nothing but disguised impatience with everything that blocks the satisfaction of insatiable and sinful cravings. Let us be vigilant, he admonishes, to discriminate with care between this false patience and the patience God himself provides, both the patience of the spirit and the patience of the flesh—the virtue in its twin forms as humility and asceticism.

In several ways Tertullian was a genuine pioneer whose work decisively shaped the later development of the western

Christian tradition. The influence of this particular treatise was greatly magnified because it served as the model for another essay on the same topic that was written in the same city by Cyprian half a century later. *The Good of Patience* expresses his conviction that not only is patience at the center of Christian discipleship, it is also one of the principal perfections of the divine nature. Patience affords the fundamental perspective for understanding the redemptive work of Christ and provides a principle of interpretation for reading the entirety of the biblical narrative. Patience has its beginning in God, in his nature and manifold activities, but it is only in the ministry and suffering of Jesus that its full dimensions are revealed.

It is the reality of the church which, to Cyprian's eyes, is the ultimate testimony to the depths of God's patience in at least two ways. The consummation of all things awaits the completion of the mission of the church, so that all people may have an opportunity to hear the proclamation of the gospel. The judgment that the sinner deserves is repeatedly postponed by the "long-enduring patience of God" in order to afford time for repentance. Furthermore, the church, whose continuing vocation tells the story of God's patience, also bears witness to it in another way. There is no one anywhere who is necessarily excluded from the embrace of the Son, whose forbearance means that he "will even receive his murderers if they are converted and come to Him. . . . What can be called more patient, what more kind? Even he who shed the blood of Christ is given life by the blood of Christ."[11] So the patience of God is not only a part of the church's proclamation, it is proclaimed simply by the existence of the redeemed community.

Cyprian uses the polarity of patience and impatience in a more or less systematic way as an interpretive device for his reading of the whole Genesis saga and the books that follow. It functions as a compass, a point of reference to illuminate the

continuities among apparently diverse narratives. In this he goes much further than Tertullian. All the patriarchs, prophets, and sages who were types and forerunners of the Christ "treasured nothing in the estimation of their virtues more than the fact that they preserved patience with a strong and stable equanimity."[12] He cites Abel and Abraham, Jacob and Joseph and Moses, as well as Isaac, whose life singularly prefigured the advent of Christ as the sacrifice for sin, and especially David, from whom Jesus was descended according to the flesh. Thus the patience revealed in the acts of God structures and sharpens our comprehension of all the biblical narrative, while impatience is shown to be the very heart and center of rebellion, both human and demonic. If Cyprian is not entirely prepared to echo Tertullian's unqualified equation of impatience with original sin, he certainly stresses with great vigor their kinship. Adam and Cain and Esau, each in his different way, were all led astray by impatience. It was the crime of impatience that first drew the whole people of Israel away from God:

> When they could not bear the delay of Moses speaking with God they dared to demand profane gods, and...always impatient of the divine teaching and guidance, by killing all their prophets and all just men, they hastened to the cross and to the shedding of the blood of the Lord.[13]

Impatience always insists that we need not share. It claims that time and space are mine instead of yours or ours together, a birthright rather than a gift, a possession and not an arena for mutuality and the exercise of stewardship. Patience, however, never ceases to acknowledge that each of us is no more than a creature, a tenant, and one among a great many. Impatience is not only faithless but ultimately hopeless, because it deprives the self of anywhere to turn for help. Neither faith nor hope has

any substance if it is not fortified by patience, which is the sole virtue that promotes the growth of hope and "ensures our perseverance as sons of God while we imitate the patience of the Father." As for love, Cyprian warns,

> Take patience away from it, and thus forsaken, it will not last. . . . Neither unity nor peace can be preserved unless brothers cherish one another with mutual forbearance and preserve the bond of unity, with patience as intermediary.[14]

Without patience, there is no virtue of any sort, no possibility for a true church, not even an enduring community—nothing at all.

With the waning of the original eschatological expectations of the Christian community of Cyprian's day, the virtue of patience inevitably gained new importance and received more careful scrutiny. Far from inevitable, however, was the fact that theologians like Cyprian would examine its different dimensions—forbearance, perseverance, endurance, and expectation—in such a compelling fashion. Patience is ascribed to the Father as one of the great divine perfections and to the Son as the secret of his messiahship. Throughout Cyprian writes as a churchman and not as a philosopher, as a pastor responsible for one of Africa's largest and most important Christian communities. His concern is for the strengthening of the family of God during a time of much difficulty and confusion, persecution and schism. Nevertheless, in *The Good of Patience* he has written not only a tract for his own times but one of the minor classics in the history of early Christian thought. It still retains its power to challenge and teach us even when such perils, at least in the forms in which Cyprian encountered them, seem long gone.

Augustine of Hippo's *On Patience* is a very slender exercise in comparison. It confines itself to two questions: where does Christian patience come from and what is its character? The most distinctive aspects of his essay are the rigor and elaborateness of his argument and the sophistication and richness of his biblical exegesis compared to those who wrote before him. Augustine argues that patience has but a single source, the free and unmerited grace of God, and defines patience as that which helps us "endure evils with equanimity so as not to abandon, through a lack of equanimity, the good through which we arrive at the better." But calm and faithful endurance is a theme that gathers about itself a cluster of associated ideas: forbearance, expectation, and perseverance. "The patient," he continues, "who prefer to bear wrongs without committing them rather than to commit them by not enduring them, both lessen what they suffer in patience and...do not destroy the good which is great and eternal."[15] Through a forbearance that has no thought of punishment or revenge, those who are patient neither permit an injury to become an obsession even more painful than the original hurt, nor do they retaliate, which would cancel out the difference between themselves and those who harm them. Leave judgment to God, counsels Augustine, revisiting terrain explored by Tertullian and Cyprian that becomes a motif in the work of virtually every later writer on patience. Leave judgment to God lest you yourself be found wanting because you have yielded to the stirrings of impatience.

Augustine knows very well that ambition, reputation, wealth, and other worldly ends can all inspire patient labor and heroic endurance, but he insists that people who persevere in pursuit of such unworthy goals find no merit before God. Authentic patience, he writes, "is the attendant of wisdom, not the handmaid of passion." The two attitudes can be to all appearances identical but, springing from different causes, they are as different as day and night. True patience is recognized only through its cause. When we are patient in a good cause, one that is untainted by passion or egotism, we are practicing true patience. Augustine develops the contrast between Adam and Job not only to juxtapose patience to the impatience that denies God's sovereignty, but also to distinguish between false patience and true. In the first, the self is enslaved by its passions; in the second, it has put the passions to flight. While Adam's pride and impatience overwhelm the humility that would have checked his "bold appetite for pleasures," Job's wisdom sustains the "humble endurance of difficulties" that so forcefully confounds his proud and foolish friends. Because of his faithfulness and patience, therefore, "instead of the things which he lost, he possessed Him who took them all away, in whom he discovered what had never perished."[16]

These reflections on Job introduce Augustine's summary of biblical precepts on patience, where he reiterates the notions of endurance and humility with all the force of a litany. Humility and patience are inseparable, just as are pride and impatience. They are rooted in contrasting loves, the love of self to the contempt of God and the love of God to the contempt of self. The first glories in the strength of its patience; the second knows that all strength which is admirable is a gift from God. "The true patience of the just," Augustine writes, "is from the same source as the charity of God which is in them, and the false patience of the unjust is from the same source as their lust of the world." As God judges the matter, there is little difference between the patience and impatience of the sinner, for they are equally infected by pride, which is the sin of the

rich. The contrast between rich and poor has nothing to do with worldly goods, but is another way to phrase the distinction between the proud and the humble. People who in their own estimation are rich are "those who disdain being needy before the Lord" and who therefore glory in their own false patience instead of praying for God's grace. The poor in spirit humbly acknowledge their own unfitness for salvation and rely on God, who alone is wealthy, for the heavenly patience that is utterly alien to the "false patience of the proud." The contrasts between the two loves—humility and pride, rich and poor, Adam and Job, passion and wisdom—are all mutually reinforcing ways through which to illuminate all that true patience means.[17]

In one way or another the virtue of patience figures in many of Augustine's writings, but as perseverance it is especially prominent in the treatises written after 425 and most notably in *On the Gift of Perseverance.* Its first section is an interpretation of the Lord's Prayer that faithfully reproduces the reflections of Cyprian on the same topic nearly two centuries earlier in a profoundly influential work. Cyprian's essay was so widely esteemed that such respected figures as Hilary of Poitiers and Ambrose of Milan confessed they were unable to add anything of significance to what the bishop of Carthage had composed. Since Cyprian depended in large measure upon his own teacher, Tertullian, just as Augustine in his turn builds upon Cyprian, there is a sense in which this portion of *On the Gift of Perseverance* represents a distillation of the thought of the three most highly regarded Latin theologians on a subject of particular importance.

Augustine begins by arguing that every petition save one in the Lord's Prayer is an appeal for the gift of perseverance, which is precisely what we can never attain for ourselves. This is the sum and substance of the Lord's Prayer: the humble request for

patience, for the unsurpassably great grace of the perseverance that will sustain faith until life is done. When we pray first of all, "Hallowed be Thy name," we are asking "that we, who were sanctified in baptism, may persevere in that which we have begun to be." The prayer that "Thy kingdom come" is a request for the same gift: "What do they who are already holy pray for, save that they may persevere in that holiness which has been given them? For not otherwise will the Kingdom of God come to them." The third petition reinforces the two that precede it, because it too appeals to God for the perseverance "which assuredly even the saints, who do the will of God, seek when they say in prayer, "Thy will be done."[18]

In his interpretation of the fourth request, "Give us this day our daily bread," Augustine relies upon an argument that Cyprian may well have learned from Tertullian. While "daily bread" also refers to bodily sustenance, for Cyprian its primary meaning is Jesus Christ himself, who is the bread of life. So this eucharistic request is also fundamentally a prayer for perseverance, asking that no temptation or lapse deprive the believer of his or her daily place at the holy table, praying "that we who are in Christ, and daily receive the Eucharist for the food of salvation, may not by the interposition of some heinous sin be separated from Christ's body." And the final two petitions of the Lord's Prayer, Augustine concludes, are also prayers for perseverance in holiness.[19]

But the fifth petition, "Forgive us our trespasses," is another matter, for it is not perseverance that is asked for. If this particular form of patience is absent, however, another equally important variety lies at its center. Cyprian illustrates the request for forgiveness by the story of the ungrateful servant who begged his master to exercise forbearance until he could repay the debt he owed, but who then displayed no forbearance toward another servant who owed him a lesser sum—and so

forfeited his forgiveness. We might hesitate to agree with Cyprian and Augustine that in the Lord's Prayer scarcely anything else is asked of the Father except perseverance, but patience in one form or another is at the heart of every petition—the request for the blessing of his patience and, by his grace, the hope of ours. The church is itself a mixed body, comprising both the faithful and the faithless. Their unlikeness can be phrased in many ways, but it is characteristic of Augustine to assert that the difference is patience, in the form of perseverance.

Patience is not a secondary virtue, a mere acolyte to others that play more important roles, but indispensable for the realization of any virtue at all. For, Augustine writes, faith without perseverance is unavailing; it cannot confer life because faith itself will die. To such a great extent does one gift of God depend upon another—first patience upon the faith and love that can be kindled by God alone, and then faith and love in their turn upon the patience that only God can provide. Tertullian and Cyprian would greet Augustine's claims with their own "Amen." Together, these three ask every generation after them whether Christian ethics can be faithfully written for any age if patience, God's and ours, is not at the center of everything.

Chapter Four

In Imitation of Christ

Gregory, Thomas Aquinas, and Thomas à Kempis

The three great Latin theologians who labored in North Africa provided the Christian community with the essentials of an understanding of patience as central both for Christian discipleship and for interpreting the ways of God with the world. When the early church suffered persecution, the ultimate expression of faith and love for God was martyrdom, and patient perseverance was the divinely given virtue it exemplified. When such days were long gone, the cultivation of patience could crown even the most ordinary and unremarkable life with a form of "unbloody martyrdom" that united the believer with the exemplary saints of earlier times.

There are many scattered references to Job in early Christian literature, but they scarcely explain why the patience of Job became the indispensable key for Christian interpretations of human suffering. How did his trials come to be understood by the church as a rehearsal of the passion of Christ? What brought this story from the periphery to the

center of the biblical narrative, as Christians understood it? The answer lies with Gregory I, the first of the great medieval popes, who more than anyone else managed to weave the threads of patience so vividly into the design of the medieval tapestry of faith. The impact of Gregory's writings upon the centuries after him was massive; no one except Augustine exerted such influence. Gregory was not a theologian of the very first rank, but he was an incomparable churchman and pastor to pastors. It was he who assumed responsibility for the secular fortunes of the shattered city of Rome, arranging for the transport of the daily necessities its citizens required.

The importance of patience did not depend solely upon the work of Gregory, of course. Other factors included the continuing development of monasticism, for which patience was the antidote to the boredom with well-doing, or *acedia,* that could afflict the cloister; the flourishing of mysticism; and the impact of the Renaissance, with its interest in classical antiquity, particularly Stoic philosophy. Popular piety was another factor—patience was both a more accessible and more interesting virtue than justice or temperance. The scholastics' interest in theological systematization and categorization, particularly that of Thomas Aquinas, played a part, and so did the importance of iconography, the church's most successful strategy for teaching in an unlettered age. Cathedrals and abbeys were sermons in stone as well as centers of worship. But there was no individual more important than Pope Gregory in linking the tribulations of Job with the passion of Christ.

Gregory wrote two works of particular significance. The first, *Pastoral Care,* is a manual for pastors, detailing what their character should be and how they should proclaim the gospel to those in their charge. As a *regula* or "rule" for the secular clergy, its influence for hundreds of years was comparable to that of the Benedictine rule for monastics, and displayed the same

extraordinary common sense. The other significant work is his lengthy commentary on Job, which is not simply an interpretation of one book of the Bible, but a comprehensive statement of Christian theology, morality, and devotional practices. It is not quite accurate to claim that this is the very first Christian commentary on the book of Job, but its few predecessors were brief and fragmentary, altogether incomparable either in ambition or influence. Gregory himself referred to Job as "this obscure work, which hitherto has been treated thoroughly by none before us." So this first extensive Christian interpretation of the patience of Job is Gregory's major contribution to the history of the virtue. Certainly he built on foundations laid long before him—by Augustine, for example—but it was in no small part because of his own influence and authority that medieval reflections thereafter were informed by the assumption that the mystery of suffering could best be explored in the light of the trials of Job and the patience he maintained.

Job is a twofold "type"—by which Gregory means a prototype or preliminary sketch, not merely a forerunner. He is a type of the suffering Son of God and also a type of the church militant, Christ's Body. It was the design of providence that Job "should by his life be a sign of Him whom by voice he proclaimed…and should so much the more truly foretell the mysteries of His Passion, who prophesied them not merely with his lips but also by suffering."[1] Like Christ in his agony, Job in his suffering is utterly alone, a just and pious man who has seemingly been abandoned even by the Lord. Bereft of his ten children and all their families, betrayed by his closest friends because of their insensitive and arrogant pretensions, betrayed even by the one closest to him of all, his wife—for hers is the voice of the temptress, urging him to curse God for the loss of everything that he has held dear—Job is steadfast still.

Certainly the influence of Gregory's commentary on Job reflects its accessibility, for it is full of aphorisms and illustrations that could be incorporated into homilies intended for ordinary parishes. Gregory is writing for the church, not the academy, and what commends his book most persuasively is its simple common sense. In the days of your loss, Gregory counsels, remember the times before you possessed what you have lost and hardly missed it, and then your grief will be assuaged. When you suffer deprivations, remember also the magnitude of all the blessings you have received from the Creator, so that you keep your loss in perspective. Patience is a matter not only of enduring the troubles of the moment, but also of banishing them from memory so that they do not fester there and breed a desire for revenge. Time can be a great healer if we will let it.

Suffering from recurrent ill health, which may have been a consequence of the severe regimen to which he subjected himself as a monk, Gregory tells us that "perhaps it was the design of divine providence that, afflicted thus, I should expound Job who was also thus afflicted, and that I should, under the lash, the better understand the mind of him who was also lashed."[2] It is clear, therefore, that the primary meaning of patience for Gregory is the calm and uncomplaining endurance of misfortune. But he also writes of its other meanings—our expectant waiting for the realization of God's kingdom, the importance of perseverance and, with special charm and persuasiveness, of its significance as forbearance, which he yokes with humility. The virtue of humility is evident when we bear with patience the injury that is done to us, remembering the injuries that others have borne because of us. As for expectant waiting, Gregory was persuaded, in the light of all the disarray in the greatest city the world had ever known, that the end was at hand and the return of Christ would free him from

the burdens of responsibility for a society that had simply fallen into pieces. Patience knows that "the mind feels the ills of the present life the more severely, in proportion as it neglects to take account of the good that comes after."[3] Not only in great matters, however, but even in everyday affairs the present is irradiated by patience—the expectation that somehow tomorrow will be better than today.

Gregory's conviction that "patience is the root and guardian of all the virtues" was cited countless times in the succeeding centuries in the theology, moral treatises, homilies, and other devotional writings of the church. Because circumstances compelled him to serve as a civil as well as an ecclesiastical administrator, he was keenly aware of the importance of patience even in secular society. Where it is absent, every form of human community comes unstitched and eventually disintegrates. "He who is indifferent to observe patience, soon gives up a social life from impatience.... For he foregoes to do good deeds of his own, who refuses to bear evil deeds of others."[4] Far from signifying passivity, patience is the catalyst without which we shall not engage in productive activity. There is a strict correlation between the decline of patience and the loss of the capacity for action; they flourish together and wither in isolation.

The universe that God has made is a hierarchy. The body is subordinate to the soul and the soul to reason; when reason is properly employed, it serves the dictates of the virtues. This perfection of our nature "springs out of patience," as Gregory explains in his exegesis of Job 4:6, "Where is thy fear, thy strength, thy patience, and the perfectness of thy ways?" These are the four stages of discipleship: the fear of the Lord is the beginning of wisdom and it leads to strength in adversity. Such strength is victorious when it is expressed in the patience that can endure every misfortune with an untroubled heart.

Patience achieves "perfectness" when as forbearance it reaches out to embrace neighbors despite all of their frailties. "Hence Truth says in the Gospel, *In your patience possess ye your souls.*"[5]

Such patience means displaying love toward our tormentors rather than merely enduring their faults and whatever they do to us, for there is no perfect patience that is not a work of love. No one is perfect except those who feel no impatience toward the imperfections of their neighbors. More than simply wisdom gleaned from experience by a moralist of exceptional talents, Gregory's words are rooted in and sustained by a vision of the suffering Son of God who instructs us in the magnitude of his sufferings and patience so that we can find peace in our own. For more than a thousand years after Gregory, in one form or another, Christian writers and preachers repeated his assurance to those taught by Christ that even in times of prosperity and peace, "We, too, can be martyrs, without the shackles, if truly we possess our souls in patience."[6] There is no higher Christian vocation.

In *Pastoral Care* Gregory paints a grim picture of the consequences of impatience, a vice which is always found in the company of arrogance and pride. Impatience leads ineluctably to the loss of the self: "The Lord has pointed out that patience is the guardian of our estate, for He taught us to possess ourselves in it. We, therefore, realize how great is the fault of impatience, seeing that by it we lose even the possession of what we are." With impatience "there is no interior discipline of wisdom"; without patience we are deprived of our powers of deliberation. We have lost touch with the contours of reality. So men and women "are borne precipitately into many wrongs, even such as they do not intend, because, obviously, impetuosity drives the mind whither it does not wish.... By their sudden impulse they undo what with protracted labor they have built up."[7] The greatest harm that impatience can do, therefore, is not to others

but to oneself. Like some of the other vices, it can rob people of their vision so that they cannot even recognize the impatience in themselves and all of its destructive power. Finally, Gregory warns his readers that the mere appearance of patience counts for nothing. One must not grieve in one's heart for what one suffers outwardly, as though it were sufficient to mask inner turmoil behind a cheerful countenance. Such hypocrisy is repugnant to God and a denial of his providence.

There is a perennial tendency in the Christian tradition to identify the life of discipleship in large measure with the practice of a single virtue. Sometimes it is hope or humility, sometimes faith construed as orthodoxy or right belief, sometimes poverty or quietism or benevolence or asceticism or even tolerance. For Lactantius, patience was the "greatest" virtue, for Tertullian the "highest," with impatience as the source of every sin, and for Gregory it is the "root and guardian" of everything good. Cyprian and Augustine argued that the whole meaning of the Lord's Prayer is the plea that God might grant us the gift of patience. In their reflections, patience is central precisely because it is never approached in isolation from other aspects of the Christian vision.

There were always other theologians, however, less able or more doctrinaire, whose focus on one virtue led them to isolate it from others and therefore present a flawed and partial gospel. So there emerged a whole constellation of sectarian movements, some quietist and some revolutionary, others millenarian, ascetical, or boasting of esoteric knowledge. One of the great achievements of Thomas Aquinas, writing six centuries after Gregory, was his comprehensive enumeration of all the virtues and their relationships to one another to prevent

this sort of distorted emphasis. His systematic treatment of the virtues demanded a more rounded and exhaustive view of discipleship. No longer could one claim that patience alone was the greatest, highest, or root of all other virtues, nor was it legitimate to fix upon some other single virtue as the key to salvation.

This is one of the reasons why Thomas is such a seminal figure. There are few people in the intellectual history of the West who have proven themselves such daring and effective pioneers as the Dominican monk who in the thirteenth century faced a radically new and wholly secular view of the world, which he enlisted in the proclamation of the gospel. Thomas offers us in the *Summa Theologica,* along with a great deal else, a comprehensive interpretation of the idea of virtue that is rooted in both the classical and Christian worlds, in Aristotle's *Nicomachean Ethics,* and in the theology of Augustine. In the moral tradition Thomas inherited there were a number of certainties, but none more fundamental than these three: the centrality of the theological virtues of faith, hope, and love; the importance of the cardinal virtues of prudence, justice, fortitude, and temperance; and the interdependence of the virtues, as well as the links between natural achievements and supernatural gifts. He brought to these beliefs a genius for systematization that expands and enriches each of them. Perhaps this was his greatest contribution: the provision of an orderly and hierarchical universe so capacious that there is a place for everything and everything is in its place.

Temperance means mastery of the self, while courage is mastery of the self in relation to others. Justice enables others to be their own masters, while prudence brings mastery of the situation in which the self is but one ingredient. This fourfold unity of the perfections of human nature points toward a higher perfection that nature by itself cannot attain, when the divine

gifts of faith, hope, and love crown all the good that nature can achieve with the joy of surrender to the God in whom alone we can find our highest good. Before Thomas there had been little agreement about the number or nature of the "lesser" or "minor" virtues. Even if his attempt at systematic inclusiveness does not seem wholly persuasive today, its logic and breadth stand in sharp contrast to the partiality and eclecticism of those who wrote in earlier times. No longer could their omissions go unnoticed or their exaggerations unchallenged. Some virtues that are of vital significance for Christian faith, such as humility and gratitude, were not mentioned in secular treatises. In the *Nicomachean Ethics,* for example, there is no attention given to humility. Since these two are inseparable from the cardinal virtues, they have not only theological relevance but also importance for ordinary individual and social life. Where they are absent, human nature will never fulfill its own proper potential. The natural and supernatural orders are knit together in a single harmonious design, but never at the cost of ignoring their profound distinction. This is the hallmark of Thomism—the differentiation of so much from so much more without the isolation of one distinct part from another.

Fortitude, or courage, is third among the cardinal virtues, ranked before temperance but after prudence and justice because unlike them it is not oriented directly toward the good but toward controlling the.passions that can turn us away from seeking God. In the good life, passions are ruled by rational habits, or virtues. Fear is the most dangerous of the passions and the one with which fortitude is principally concerned. Courage is the middle way between the extremes of cowardice and rashness—always prudent and not proud, it heeds admonitions not to dare too much and not to take the whole weight of the world on its own shoulders. Thomas writes that the principal act of fortitude is endurance rather than aggressiveness in the

face of danger, thus echoing Cicero's comment that "fortitude is deliberate facing of dangers and bearing of toils." Above all, it is concerned with the fear of death. There is the courage that bears the fear of death in the course of grievous illness, there is the greater courage that triumphs over fear in swimming to the rescue of a drowning friend, and the greater courage still, when we are willing to sacrifice ourselves in the course of a just war, where "courage shines forth in all its purity." Only in the face of death can courage be exhibited in its most perfect form.[8]

The lesser virtues Thomas associates with courage are patience and perseverance. Patience is the endurance of difficulties, while perseverance has to do with persistence toward a goal. The former is a mean between indifference—the inability to respond in any way either to the sufferings of others or to one's own—and impatience, which Thomas describes as the refusal to endure sorrow and an immoderate attempt at self-protection. The latter is a mean between softness, too ready surrender to obstacles that we might well overcome, and pertinacity, which means excessive persistence, stubbornly clinging to our goals even after it is clear that they are inappropriate or unattainable. If patience and perseverance are confined to situations that require fortitude—that is, if they are displayed in the face of the danger of death and express the individual's mastery of the fear of dying—then they will be an integral part of a major virtue. However, if these virtues are displayed in the face of any other kind of hardship, where there is no actual threat of death, they are no longer part of a cardinal virtue, but subordinate, "annexed thereto as secondary to the principal." In either event, one can no longer claim patience as the root and guardian of all the virtues, the greatest among them.[9]

These distinctions between greater and lesser virtues are simply one example of the extraordinarily rich process of

discrimination by which Aquinas maps the moral landscape in a more detailed and meticulous way than any of his predecessors. Moving from greater to lesser, he locates the position of patience as he sees it with remarkable precision. Courage and patience themselves differ not only because they are concerned with different kinds of endurance, the first with the danger of death and the second with any other kind of evil. They also differ because one has to do mainly with fear and the other with grief. "Fortitude is chiefly about fear," Thomas writes, "while patience is chiefly about sorrow." We are said to be patient not simply because we do not flee from a bad situation, but because we suffer the things that hurt us "here and now, in such a way as not to be inordinately saddened by them."[10] After fear, grief is perhaps the passion with the greatest power to keep us from pursuing the good. Patience is profoundly important, therefore, as our defense against the distractions of dejection and sorrow and the frustrations that seem to have no end in sight.

Thomas discusses perseverance in a separate and independent question. It is not a part of patience, although the two are certainly companions and allies. Perseverance is required everywhere and always, for there is not a single virtuous pursuit in which success can be achieved without consistency and persistence. It deals with whatever difficulties are inherent in the situation. Patience and perseverance are both moral and not theological virtues—that is to say, they are not given by God but acquired by human effort, natural rather than supernatural—but Aquinas asks nonetheless whether they can be fully realized apart from the grace of God. His answer is that neither can. When patience endures the loss of all things because it will not forsake the Good this world cannot give, or when perseverance persists no matter how great the cost because of its devotion to the Source of life, the natural virtues are transformed by faith, hope, and love: natural

aspirations are satisfied by a gift that nature itself cannot attain. In the end, therefore, "it is clearly impossible to have patience without the help of grace."[11] As natural virtues, patience and perseverance each has its own real independence; as elements in the Christian life, however, they are reunited in their shared dependence as empty vessels awaiting the gift of God's grace.

It seems almost inevitable that Thomas' attempt to create a unified theory that is at the same time so all-encompassing and so detailed, from traditions as disparate as the classical and the biblical, should foster a number of awkwardnesses and anomalies. One problem is that his integration of some virtues with others also leads to their segregation from still others, even though such a consequence may not be intended at all. For example, there is the way that Thomas annexes humility, gratitude, and patience to the principal virtues—humility to temperance, gratitude to justice, and patience to fortitude. But it is by no means obvious that humility belongs with temperance rather than justice, or equally with both, or that patience is merely one dimension of fortitude rather than integral to all the cardinal virtues in equal measure.

This raises a second problem that is no less acute. The *Summa* is full of citations of other authorities, especially Aristotle, Cicero, Augustine, and Gregory. Thomas is profoundly conscious of himself as the inheritor of a great tradition. His passion for clarity and concern for precise definition are at odds with a certain messiness and untidiness that characterize the theologians who preceded him. At the same time, his achievement obscures an important truth. In earlier commentators this very untidiness and the ambiguities it contained served to express an almost unmanageable richness within the ideas themselves, a welter of meanings and connotations that it is beyond the power of our language to define and isolate in any tidy fashion. Thus when Thomas

identifies patience only with a particular kind of endurance, and excludes the ideas of forbearance and expectant waiting that were central to the early church and the Bible, we have losses as well as gains. Thomas' contributions to the tradition of moral virtue are enormous and lasting, but at the same time they were bought at a price. They have a certain rigidity and artificiality that always remained in tension with the messiness and untidiness that are part of our perennial condition. Virtue has a life that anatomical studies cannot wholly comprehend.

Alongside the scholastic appetite for system and classification, however, older traditions not only continued but flourished. The mystical piety of Francis of Assisi and Bernard of Clairvaux, for example, was expressed anew by Aquinas' own closest friend, Bonaventure. Throughout the Middle Ages patience was a fundamental theme in theology and ethics as well as a recurrent figure in art, iconography, and popular piety. The contemplative tradition understood it well: somehow the notion of patience captured the mystery of the work of Christ in a way that nothing else could quite match. The self is both an actor and a reactor. We act but we are acted upon by others. Patience, sometimes a virtue but always a condition no one can long avoid, captures this dimension of creaturely life as an ideal and an inescapable reality. For writers such as Thomas à Kempis, the story of Jesus Christ testified that this "passive" side of selfhood lay at the very center of the secret of redemption. In Christ's passion all the virtues seemed to coalesce in measureless patience, ever persevering, enduring and forbearing even toward those who condemned him to die.

It seems extraordinary that one small volume written more than half a millennium ago for a struggling monastic

community in the Lowlands, advocating renunciation of the world and no compromise with all its works and ways, should remain a widely read and well-loved devotional classic today. *The Imitation of Christ*, usually ascribed to Thomas à Kempis, is a summary of all that is best in fifteenth-century piety and the supreme expression of the temper of the *Devotio Moderna*, a movement that began in the Netherlands in the late fourteenth century. This new or "modern" devotion mined a rich and ancient tradition, for it was greatly indebted to Augustine, Bernard, Bonaventure, and many others. But it was modern in contrast to the mystical piety that had flourished in much fourteenth-century monasticism: far more skeptical of learning, focused on the will rather than the intellect, practical rather than theoretical. The movement emphasized the cultivation of the Christian virtues and took as its model the way of life of Jesus of Nazareth as it is portrayed in the four gospels. Therefore it was particularly accessible to the laity, and its houses of the Brothers and Sisters of the Common Life were communities that required no monastic vows. It did not survive the sixteenth century as an independent movement, but continued to influence Catholic and Protestant churches in more or less equal measure and remained a vital force for corporate renewal and individual growth.

For Thomas à Kempis, the whole ministry of Jesus Christ can be summarized by two words, "He suffered." Jesus' passion was not simply the conclusion of his life but the substance of it all. The redemptive secret of such innocent suffering was his patient obedience to the will of the Father. Therefore, the imitation of Christ means, first and last and always, to take up one's own cross without complaint and to follow him upon "the royal way of the holy Cross."[12] We too must suffer; there is no life without suffering, by which Thomas à Kempis means the experience of pain and loss that is visited upon unbeliever and

disciple alike. There is nowhere to flee for refuge from adversities and afflictions too numerous to chronicle. Life means often little more than an incessant process of deprivation—of youth and health, of family and friends, of security and reputation and reason itself. The only serious question, then, is how we bear what we cannot evade: with faith or fear, assent or protest, equanimity or impatience, with Christ as our constant companion or without him, condemned to the loneliness that intensifies much suffering.

Discipleship is characterized above all else by love and by the virtues which are its inseparable companions—humility, poverty, and patience. In the end, everything depends upon whether we respond with patience in the face of what we must eventually endure no matter how many and various are the stratagems that we devise to protect ourselves from misfortune. The legacy of Adam is our egocentric, impatient, and rebellious will. The principal task of patience is the cultivation of an ascetical outlook, which "mortifies" the will and teaches us to die away from this world, so that we can endure without discontent the loss of all things for the sake of fellowship with Christ. If patience cannot restrain and purify the fallen will, there is neither health in us nor hope for us. This virtue is woven into the texture of Thomas' entire work, chapter after chapter. But endurance without complaint would be impossible because of the weight of our sin and the magnitude of our adversities, were it not for the forbearance that can disarm the assaults upon us. Forbearance allows us to move on to other and better things: our expectant waiting for the new heaven and earth, which affords us some greater perspective upon our present misfortunes, and the perseverance that can sustain us even when God withholds his consolation in the midst of the trials ordained for us to undergo.

Thomas à Kempis typically relies not on a complex theological vocabulary but on the personal language of friendship and love. He prefers to write of Christ as the companion whose sturdy support enables us to endure what would be prove unbearable for an individual alone.

> It is said in proverbs and by many that to have a companion in suffering is a comfort to the miserable. Who is this companion so kind and good, and who knows how to have compassion on the miserable and afflicted? This is our Lord Jesus Christ.

Companionship is a basic motif in *The Imitation of Christ*, which takes the form of a dialogue and stresses the contemporaneity of Jesus in every age. Were this not so, Jesus could never confer upon us that gift of patience we cannot attain for ourselves:

> Make that possible for me, O Lord, by grace, which appears impossible to me by nature. Thou knowest how little I am able to bear, and how soon I am cast down, when a slight trouble arises.

In one of the many dialogues concerning patience that mark the companionship of Christ and the disciple, Jesus says:

> Son, I came down from Heaven for thy salvation; I took upon Myself thy miseries, not from necessity but drawn by love, that you may learn to be patient and to bear meekly the miseries of this life. For from the home of My birth, even to My death upon the Cross, I was never free from sorrow.

Should the servant fare better than his lord? No, says Thomas, the best we can do is imitate Christ in his patience, "for Thy life is our way, and by holy patience we advance towards Thee."[13]

All companionship requires patience. Companionship with Jesus, however, offers as a gift what it also requires, so that by

grace we are drawn into the likeness of the giver. As we have seen in other contexts, here is one more fundamental motif that must figure in a constructive account of patience: the way that patience is both required by and anchored in the very nature of those for whom life is mutuality and companionship, conversation and dialogue.

Thomas is adamant in portraying this world as a sea of troubles. Earthly security is an illusion; ease and comfort are fleeting and leave those who enjoy them even less prepared for the deprivations and disappointments that never lie far in the future. But we endlessly compound our pain by trying to escape it, for then "the anxiety to escape tribulation will continually attend you." Every impatient complaint at the injustice of our lot simply reinforces its torment. Fixation upon the suffering and anguish we endure does nothing except augment the pain and cloud our vision until our minds can encompass none of the other realities that might place our anguish in perspective and render it less incapacitating. There is nowhere for the impatient soul to go, nothing to do, no place to hide, no hope of help, no solace anywhere in the world. The pursuit of treasures on earth is folly, for they provide no defense against disease, age, frailty, and death. "The Cross, then, is always at hand," Thomas writes,

> and everywhere awaits you. You cannot escape it, run where you will; for wherever you go, you take yourself with you, and you will always find yourself. Look above you, look below you, look without and within you, and everywhere you will find the cross; and it is necessary that you exercise patience everywhere. . . . If you bear it unwillingly, you will make it burdensome, and increase its pressure, yet notwithstanding you will have to bear it. If you cast away one cross, you will doubtless find another, and perhaps a heavier one.[14]

For the companion of Christ, however, the way of the cross is the only path to salvation. Our faith, strengthened by the conviction that all things are in accordance with the will of God, reaches out to embrace all these misfortunes as tests and trials and occasions for growth. They are expressions of God's justice, opportunities for the practice of uncomplaining endurance and forbearance, and instruction in the virtue of humility and the need for repentance. Misfortune counsels all those who are struggling to avoid it that "there is greater merit in suffering than in doing."[15] In other words, God calls us first of all to be *patients*—dependent, exposed, no longer in control of our own situation. This theme, too, is crucial for a constructive account of patience and we must explore its Christological foundation. The companionship of the risen Christ can confer peace even in the midst of darkness; it can provide gladness where there has been a wasteland of pain and loss. Because of the transformative power that the grace of patience exerts, changing all that it touches into the very opposite of what it seems, the initiative of the sufferer can be immensely effective. Apparent curses become eventual blessings.

Commentators on Thomas à Kempis have frequently and correctly written of his presentation of the gospel as a message of world-renunciation. But this description is appropriate only if one immediately adds the qualification *for Christ's sake*. There is no hatred or disparagement of the world in *The Imitation of Christ*. We do not have creation as it came fresh from the Father's hand, but only as it has been disfigured and spoiled by sin. But it is still God's world, and that is the reason why its attractions appeal so powerfully. Three features characterize Thomas' renunciation of the world for Christ. The first is its eschatological orientation, by which every earthly tie must be subordinated for the sake of what is to come. Second, renunciation is Christ-centered. It is motivated not by dismay

at the world's coarse and brutal ways, but by love for the crucified. Finally, it is disciplinary: we must be purified of the sin of Adam's fall. We must die to this world and all its incentives toward a life of disobedience. The world must be renounced if the will is to be healed.

Such world-renunciation contains no impulse whatsoever toward solitariness. After all, Thomas à Kempis was a monastic who wrote for the strengthening of the community of which he was a member. The theme of companionship emerges anew. Patience is the source and the product of companionship; in one's relationship to Christ, the divine patience is creative of the human. So it is also in all Christian relationships; patience is the root and the fruit of companionship. Thomas' work everywhere reflects a profound sense of the interdependence of human lives, of the mutuality and reciprocity that are necessary for our life together to thrive:

> God has so ordained it, that we should learn to bear one another's burdens, for there is no one who has not some defect, no one without some burden, no one independent of others, no one wise enough of himself; but we ought to bear with one another, comfort one another, help, instruct, and advise one another.[16]

We are members one of another, fellow sojourners and pilgrims, participants in a diverse community that spans many ages and embraces many lands. Companionship has to do not only with Christ and one's contemporaries, but also with the relationship between the church militant and the church triumphant, the earthly and heavenly aspects of a single community. In times of hardship and distress, Christians can find solace in the stories of saints and martyrs who surmounted even greater obstacles and suffered still crueler deprivations to attain the kingdom of God. Thomas' sense of our dependence

upon one another and on all the generations that preceded ours is complemented by his insistence upon the crucial need for forbearance. Forbearance comes on the heels of genuine self-knowledge. If we are aware of all our own faults and idiosyncrasies, which we expect others to tolerate and excuse, we can scarcely fail to accept in them what is so transparent in ourselves. Indeed, Thomas writes,

> If I rightly saw myself, I could not say that any creature had ever unjustly treated me; and therefore I cannot justly complain before Thee. But because I have frequently and grievously sinned against Thee, every creature may rightly take arms against me.[17]

Forbearance will never dwindle to mere permissiveness or indifference so long as we acknowledge that Christ alone is the mirror in whom we can see ourselves—both as we are and as we are intended to become. We shall know nothing of our true selves apart from him whose forbearance is the model for our own. "Strive to be patient in bearing the defects of others," Thomas advises. "You yourself have many also, and they have to put up with them. If you are not yourself such as you would wish to be, how can you expect to find another according to your liking?"[18] He stresses that we must show forbearance toward ourselves as well as others; we must be patient and not have impossible expectations of ourselves. Each of his exhortations to stand firm and endure valiantly seems to be accompanied by a renewed sense of the self's frailty, even though upheld by grace. If we are too harsh when we look at ourselves in the mirror, the end will be paralysis and despair. Patience with one's own self is an often neglected but very important aspect of a constructive account of patience, especially in a culture so prone to evaluate in terms of what we have accomplished and the positions we have held.

Thomas certainly does not advise us to ignore our own faults and weaknesses, but he emphasizes that the saints also endured periods of spiritual dryness when they could find no consolation and seemed condemned not only to suffer, but to suffer alone. Such forlorn, arid times are the occasional daily bread of most ordinary Christians, and one can find comfort in the knowledge that even saints and martyrs have experienced something similar yet persevered and were consoled. The companionship of Christ is constant, but that is not always apparent to us, especially when our eyes are clouded by despair. "All is not lost," Thomas counsels, "because you feel yourself very often tried or much tempted. You are man, and not God; you are flesh, and not an Angel. How can you expect always to remain in the same degree of virtue?" Progress in the spiritual life depends not so much on feelings of devotion and comfort as it does on "bearing their withdrawal with humility, self-sacrifice, and patience."[19]

Medieval monasticism and the mysticism that flourished within it developed over the course of centuries, assuming many and various forms and producing a great range of literature. There is nothing in this literature, however, that quite matches the beauty and power of *The Imitation of Christ* as an expression of the Christian devotional life. Thomas à Kempis was neither an innovator nor a great speculative intellect. It is the simplicity, the personalism, and the pastoral concern of his work that have placed it in the vanguard of the classics of Christian faith. Furthermore, few others have written as eloquently of the centrality of patience in the life of Christ himself, or as a key for understanding what discipleship entails, or for the transformation of the pain and deprivations of existence into ties that bind believers inseparably in companionship with their Risen Lord. With Thomas à Kempis, companionship becomes another motif in the discussion of

Christian patience, the patience that Christ both confers and requires in our relationships with our neighbors if all people are to dwell together in harmony. Elsewhere Thomas writes that "the garments of Jesus are humility, poverty in things even necessary, patience in adversity, and perseverance in virtue."[20] Humility, poverty, patience, and perseverance—these are the virtues that are always and everywhere the companions of love.

Chapter Five

"The Slowness of the Good"

John Calvin, Jeremiah Burroughs, and Søren Kierkegaard

In 1737 Jonathan Edwards, the greatest theologian America has ever produced, prepared sixteen meditations for his congregation in Northampton, Massachusetts, on the hymn to Christian love in Paul's first letter to the Corinthians. *Charity and its Fruits* is one of his simplest and most attractive works, and its final meditation is about patience in the form of perseverance. There Edwards develops the theme of true and counterfeit grace in terms of perseverance. While true grace transforms the innermost nature of the sinner, its counterfeit is superficial; it excites the emotions but leaves the will untouched. Therefore perseverance is a gift it has no power to confer. Under the covenant of works, which existed from Adam to Christ, Edwards argues, our only possibility of perseverance depended on our own obedience to God's law,

whereas under the covenant of grace perseverance comes through our participation in the perfect obedience of the Son of God, the exemplar of every variety of patience. The covenant of grace, Edwards argues, "was introduced to supply what was wanting in the first covenant, and a sure ground of perseverance was the main thing that was wanting in it."[1]

The redeeming work of Christ is not merely the restoration and repair of what has been broken, but a fresh creative act. Reconciliation brings to the human situation something new—not only a recovery of what is lost, but a genuine addition. What is added is patience, Christ's and ours. Before the coming of Jesus Christ, sinners as well as saints were aware of some of the forms of patience—life in a fallen and often hostile world is simply unimaginable without it, if only to serve our own ambitions for security and power. But with Christ comes the gift of grace, patience in a radically new mode, which Edwards called "necessary perseverance." He asserts that the real difference between the covenants of grace and works, between revelation in Christ and all other revelations, is the gift of patience, or perseverance. Today such a sweeping claim may seem strange indeed, but it was not his own invention. Augustine had said much the same and it was powerfully reaffirmed in the tradition of the Protestant Reformation that had its origin in John Calvin.

The subject of the *Institutes of the Christian Religion,* Calvin's great work in systematic theology published in its definitive edition in 1559, is simply God's revelation in Jesus Christ. Calvin interprets the whole drama of his life and death and resurrection from the perspective of the three anointed offices of the Old Testament—prophecy, priesthood, and kingship—which together constitute the meaning of messiah, "anointed one." Jesus is the last and greatest of prophets because he is himself the word that he bears. He is the last and

greatest of priests because he is himself the sacrifice that he offers. He is the last and greatest of kings because his kingship is perfected through patient obedience in the suffering that discloses the Father's gracious will.

It is impossible to understand Calvin's ideas on patience without looking at his notion of providence, which governs not only all human affairs but all things whatsoever. Calvin speaks of God's omnipotence as "a watchful, effective, active sort, engaged in ceaseless activity....He so regulates all things, that nothing takes place without his deliberation."[2] Providence encompasses the future as well as the past and reveals God's concern for all of humanity but most especially for the church. Sometimes God's providence works through secondary causes or intermediaries, sometimes apart from them, and sometimes against them. Within this universe that is created, sustained, and ruled by the providence of God, there is no room whatsoever for the intervention of fortune or chance, fate or accident or caprice. The distinction between divine willing and divine permission is simply an invention of philosophers; Calvin scorns it. That does not mean, however, that it is possible even for those who have been redeemed in Christ to decipher the ultimate significance of events, for their perspectives are limited and their vision still obscured by sin. To pretend to see as God sees is presumption and Calvin warns us to be vigilant against this sort of zealousness. Much will remain obscure until our pilgrimage is done.

For Calvin the doctrine of providence means that patience will always be the sum and substance of the Christian life. The freedom from anxiety and fear that a sense of God's providence bestows sets us free to commit ourselves "fearlessly" to God.[3] Faith in God's providence is the Christian's greatest solace and comfort, the surest source of strength, and the only certain remedy for the despair that threatens when the ways of the world seem too callous and abusive for us to bear. If all that we receive comes from God alone, and God is our Father by our adoption in Christ, then our situation is itself transformed. The focus of our attention is no longer what has been done to us, or those who have inflicted the hurt. For example, Calvin says,

> If Joseph had stopped to dwell upon his brothers' treachery, he would never have been able to show a brotherly attitude toward them. But since he turned his thoughts to the Lord, forgetting the injustice, he inclined to gentleness and kindness, even to the point of comforting his brothers and saying: "It is not you who sold me into Egypt, but I was sent before you by God's will, that I might save your life. Indeed, you intended evil against me, but the Lord turned it into good."[4]

Even in its smallest and most commonplace details, the life of the disciple is wholly determined by the Father's sovereign will, and not his will only, but that of every living thing. So patience will always be at the heart of the Christian life—not in isolation from faith and love, of course, but at their side and in their service. The virtue of patience is thus extraordinarily prominent in Calvin's writing on the Christian life because of the unqualified and explicitly argued rigor of his interpretation of the absolute sovereignty of God.

By itself, affliction cannot produce patience or heighten our sensitivity or develop our character. Misfortune usually spawns impatience, resentment, anger, and, ultimately, despair. Its victims become ever more deeply entangled in their unhappy circumstances, because their responses to adversity chain them all the more tightly to whatever it is they have suffered. Calvin also acknowledges the existence of people who exhibit no religious commitment at all, but meet even the most terrible vicissitudes of life courageously and without complaint. In his eyes, however, such heroism has little in common with Christian faith. That is why he distinguishes so sharply between Christian and "philosophical" patience, by which he means Stoicism. Stoicism simply bows to necessity, while Christianity counsels obedience to holy personal will. Moreover, for Christians patience is the result of grace and therefore inseparable from the humility that recognizes our utter dependence upon God, while Stoic patience is a human attainment essentially bound up with pride. In freely accepting whatever necessity requires, it expresses the self's autonomy in the face of what is inevitable.

Nor do Christians share the Stoic distrust of the emotions. Instead, they are called to sympathize with the sorrows and losses suffered by others and to rejoice in their successes and happiness. Patience is not unfeeling; it renders us more sensitive and responsive to the feelings of others:

> Patiently to bear the cross is not to be utterly stupefied and to be deprived of all feeling of pain.... We have nothing to do with this iron philosophy which our Lord and Master has condemned not only by his word, but also by his example.[5]

Finally, for Calvin as for Thomas à Kempis, Christian patience comprehends the importance of community and companionship. There is no true relationship with God apart from our neighbor. We are called to show forbearance, to refrain from dealing with others as they deserve, and to offer still another chance to those who have betrayed us. Patience demands that we should bear with the weakness we discover in others and grant them whatever time and space their strengthening requires. In classical Stoicism, however, there is no such impulse to comradeship or recognition that life is mutuality. Those who stand most firmly are those who stand alone.

Calvin begins his discussion of the Christian life by insisting that faith and repentance are virtually synonymous. Repentance is not a stage in the progress of discipleship but an abiding reorientation in which the first becomes last and the last is now first. It means the conversion of all thoughts and feelings from concern with ourselves to selfless commitment to God. This penitent and faithful redirection of everything we are has two aspects, which Calvin calls mortification and vivification—the struggle against sin and the renewal of the self through its incorporation into Christ.[6] Patience is at the heart of both movements. Perhaps it is most evident in the former as forbearance and endurance, and in the latter as perseverance in faith and expectant waiting for the consummation of all things. But these are differences of emphasis rather than firm distinctions; every form of patience has its role to play in bringing each to fruition.

Mortification itself has two aspects, self-denial—which Calvin calls "the sum of the Christian life"—and bearing the cross. In a sense, they differ because the first has to do with our internal condition and the second with the adversity that visits us from without. The two are related, of course, in the struggle against self-centeredness and the evidence that the old self is, indeed, dying away from the things of this world. Self-denial and bearing the cross always serve the same end, which is growth into the likeness of Jesus Christ, "the example of self-denial and patience." Self-denial, therefore, must not be confused with temperance or moderation, for it is a truly radical reversal of orientation from sinful self-love to the hatred of the self as sinner. This sort of conversion is not accomplished once for all, not even by grace; it is a lifelong challenge to transform our instincts, our desires, and above all our reason. For Calvin, our fallen reason is the heart of our problem. Self-denial is the patient surrender of every dimension of life to God.[7]

Because self-denial means dying away from the world and its endless temptations, as well as bearing the cross, together they free us from the obsessive pursuit of wealth and power and favor in which we lose touch with ourselves. We are liberated as well from the continual anxiety that all these will someday be snatched away from us for no reason. The practice of humility awakens us to the needs of our neighbors and allows us to offer help without worrying about the cost. Because we are no longer gripped by thirst for redress or revenge, we find we can befriend people whom previously we would have turned away. Now we can turn away instead from our obsession with our own misfortunes, because, whatever happens, the disciple "will know it ordained of God."[8]

Self-denial can change the world. It can cure the selfishness of our vision and bring us into new community not only with our neighbors but with our rivals and our enemies. It can support us in the midst of misfortunes that otherwise might have overwhelmed us and recognize new possibilities within the world that our self-absorption could neither see nor grasp. Paradoxical as it may seem, self-denial can provide us with unexpected strength that otherwise we never could have found for ourselves. Therefore, even though the patience that self-denial involves is first of all the internal discipline that God inspires, so that we can turn ourselves over to the Lord, the consequences for our transactions with others and with the world are numerous beyond calculation. Although patience in some sense means submission, it cannot be equated with passivity and resignation; it is a power that can transform the world precisely because its eyes are focused upon God.

Bearing the cross is the core of patience. Because we are devoted to God, writes Calvin in language reminiscent of Thomas à Kempis, we are also devoted to suffering, for the God we serve is a sufferer whose whole life was a perpetual cross.

Every Christian must bear the cross, "for whomever the Lord has adopted and deemed worthy of his fellowship ought to prepare themselves for a hard, toilsome and unquiet life, crammed with very many and various kinds of evil."[9] Although bearing the cross is the part of mortification that has to do with endurance, if it is lacking then self-denial cannot fulfill its own aspirations. Our quest for security for ourselves and for those we love, our insatiable hungers, and our desire to make a mark or leave a memorial so greatly spoil our vision that despite our best efforts we will fail to see all that true self-denial entails. So we need the discipline of the crosses we have to bear, for they can open our eyes to understand the self-denial toward which God's grace first directed us.

Bearing the cross also has two aspects. The first is our endurance of all the apparent misfortunes that can come upon us: the loss of loved ones, or health or wealth or honor and the many other blessings of this life. The sufferings that Christians bear are no different than those of others, but the response of the disciple is expressed by the patience that, dying to this present age, seeks nothing except the grace to surrender everything to the Lord. In some part, bearing the cross is meant for our edification, shattering our self-confidence while at the same time enabling us to recognize God's presence and power in the midst of suffering. Bearing the cross tests our patience "as gold is tested in a fiery furnace," although disciples cannot "manifest any other obedience to him save what he has given them."[10] Antagonism and suffering also come to Christians for no reason other than they are members of the church, and this is the second aspect of bearing the cross. When the church is scorned, vilified, and persecuted, disciples should give thanks for the opportunity to join in the sufferings of Christ himself. Both dimensions of bearing the cross are essential elements in

the cleansing from all unrighteousness that God wills for his saints in preparation for their entry into the kingdom.

The providence of God provides each of us with a place of our own, work to which we must devote ourselves, a sense of contentment the world can never match and never overturn, and companionship with the Son of God that neither life nor death can destroy. These four themes—placement, prayer, peace, and perseverance—associated with God's providence cast additional light on patience. "Each individual," Calvin writes, "has his own kind of living assigned to him by the Lord as a sort of sentry post so that he may not heedlessly wander about throughout life."[11] For each person a definite time and place have been prepared, and this is the context in which an individual is to fulfill the will of God. The Christian's calling is inseparable from his or her placement: as the prophet Jonah learned, God can neither be served nor eluded by emigration to a foreign land. The meanings of self-denial and bearing the cross are revealed by the demands of the situation in which we have been placed. So the vocation of the Christian is to be exercised patiently wherever we finds ourselves, not deferred until we have discovered a gentler and more hospitable landscape.

In this place to which each of us has been called, commitment to Christ does not mean first of all healing the sick or feeding the poor or the creation of a just social order, although all these have their own urgent importance. The "chief exercise of faith" is the act of prayer. Prayer requires patience, for we must persevere in it. At the same time it is patience for which we must pray. Most important, in all our petitions we must express the patience that lies at the heart of self-denial and bearing the cross, lest we fall into a kind of prayer that tries to reverse the proper relationship between master and servant by making God our instrument. In the

Lord's Prayer, "before we make any prayer for ourselves, we pray that his will be done."[12] It is in our quietude and silence, not in busyness, that we draw nearest to the Lord.

For those who patiently and prayerfully pursue their calling wherever the will of God has placed them, even in the midst of struggle and failure and loss there is peace. Now we know that our true home lies elsewhere than on the earth around us. Christian patience always provides the believer with the peace the world cannot give, and the secret of this peace is the assurance that nothing can separate us from the love of God. Even though faith is a divine work, however, we can find little reason for confidence when we explore in prayer the weakness and fickleness of our own devotion. It is only when we turn entirely away from ourselves to acknowledge the sovereignty and grace of God that we find grounds for certainty and joy. What more might one ask of God than faith? For Calvin, the answer is clear: the gift of perseverance. Of what value is faith, if there is no assurance that it will accompany us all the days of our lives? "Call and faith are of little account unless perseverance be added; and this does not happen to all. But Christ has freed us from this anxiety."[13] Those who are numbered among the saints cannot fall away, because such is God's good pleasure.

Faith comes before patience, but patience is necessary for the survival of faith. Without perseverance, faith is an empty vessel, availing nothing. In his commentary on Psalm 119, Calvin refers to patience as "the chief virtue of the faithful." It furnishes much of the stone from which discipleship is quarried. Neither self-denial nor bearing the cross is intelligible without constant reference to its dimensions. Because its meaning is simply surrender to God, patience has the capacity beyond all else to transform us and the world in which we dwell. The overwhelming sense of providence active everywhere and

always, of the transformative power of the virtue, of the importance of placement and self-denial, and of the last great gift of election, necessary perseverance—these are among Calvin's most distinctive and carefully argued contributions to the discussion of Christian patience.

Calvin's influence spread far beyond Geneva, the city in which he undertook most of his work of reform, and profoundly shaped religious life in the English-speaking world on both sides of the Atlantic. In England, despite all the disagreements between defenders of the episcopacy and those who favored a presbyterian or congregational form of church government, both Puritans and high-church Anglicans shared a debt to the theology of Calvin. *The Rare Jewel of Christian Contentment,* a work that is representative of much seventeenth-century Puritan theology, was published two years after the death of Jeremiah Burroughs in 1646, when the great Nonconformist divine who had served as a member of the Westminster Assembly was at the height of his fame as a preacher in London. He was minister to two of the greatest congregations in England, Stepney and Cripplegate, where crowds came to hear sermons apparently unrivaled in popular appeal.

The subject of *The Rare Jewel* is contentment and its opposite, "murmuring." The first is a more than human achievement, the second the work of Satan, because our lives are governed for better or worse by powers greater than our own. Burroughs writes of "Christian contentment" as "that sweet, inward, quiet, gracious frame of spirit, which freely submits to and delights in God's wise and fatherly disposal in every condition." Although he describes it in a variety of rich and subtle ways, Burroughs is careful to insist that contentment remains a mystery "very hard for a carnal heart to understand."[14] It is wholly the work of God, a state of grace in which the human will clings fervently to what the intellect has been enabled to apprehend—the revelation of God in the cross and resurrection of Jesus Christ—and in which the emotions are focused and disciplined by the faithful will. Contentment involves our doing and our suffering and our whole affective life, but above all Burroughs prizes its qualities of responsiveness and patience. If contentment cannot be wholly identified with patience, the virtue is at once a crucial means for its achievement and a very large proportion of the achievement itself.

Burroughs chronicles more than a dozen ways in which such contentment remains a mystery. The first is that Christians are the most contented people in the world and at the same time the most dissatisfied—content because they patiently accept their circumstances as a blessing from God, no matter how difficult and impoverished they may be, and yet dissatisfied because not even all the delights the world can offer will assuage their thirst for God. These joys are no more than an "earnest penny," a first installment and pledge, of the glory that is to be revealed. The second mystery is that true contentment is gained by a process of subtraction and not by addition. It is not found by adding to one's possessions or accumulating new honors or extending one's sphere of dominance, but rather by reducing the range of one's needs and aspirations. A person finds peace by "subtracting from his desires, so as to make his desires and his circumstances even and equal." Such patience as this, life in conformity with the modesty of one's condition, "is a way that the world has no skill in."[15]

When Burroughs explores the patience that is the substance of such contentment, he begins by affirming that it is both an act of freedom and an expression of happiness. First, patience

reveals human initiative, not simply resignation; it is an act that affirms our situation and not mere passivity in the face of it. There can be no real freedom where we are blind to the realities of our condition. The patience of the Christian is a free act because it follows from knowledge that God reigns and there are no events he does not determine. The second point is that patience involves a reaching out to whatever comes—a willingness to embrace it no matter what it may be, to welcome it with thanksgiving. The disciple knows that in the providence of God nothing can be altered without risking a thousand other alterations and in the church all afflictions are ultimately in the service of God's redemptive purposes. In true patience there is no apprehensiveness, no misgivings or reluctance, no grimness of spirit or Stoic passionlessness. Christian patience is thanksgiving and contentment because wherever we turn we can see the wisdom of God in everything.

It is true that in surrender to God the disciple acknowledges God's sovereignty yet takes pleasure in God's wisdom, for "the Lord sees further than I do. And how do I know but that had it not been for this affliction I should have been undone?" The focus is less on God's omnipotence, as it might seem to be in Calvin, than on divine wisdom grounded in love. If patience is justified because God's wisdom is the source of every paragraph and page of our experience, then the self will let nothing ever disturb the quiet of its heart. It will practice the art of keeping silence before God, which is difficult because "not only must the tongue hold its peace; the soul must be silent." An untroubled countenance is worth nothing if inwardly we are seething with discontent. Yet such quietness and silence have nothing in common with indifference: Christian contentment is not "opposed to making in an orderly manner our moan and complaint to God, and to our friends."[16] Such sharing of our

burdens with our Father has nothing whatsoever to do with murmuring; in fact, it is a part of patience.

If we would understand the proportions of the Christian life, we must look to Christ himself, whose ministry was marked by two forms of obedience, distinct but inseparably joined, the "active" and the "passive." Both are forms of suffering. In his passive obedience, Jesus is patient unto death, suffering the wrath of God, the assaults of the powers of darkness, and the cruelties of the world. In his active obedience, he is a patient who is perfectly responsive to the Father's will. In suffering at the hands of his enemies and suffering the initiative of the Father, he is the agent of our redemption. In both kinds of obedience, patience is the foundation of everything else—not patience understood simply as one moral virtue among others, but perfect openness to the will of his Father.

Those who take up the cross in imitation of Jesus must also come to this paradox. The saints are "passive" in their activity because they depend upon the initiative of grace and its continual reinforcement; they are "active" in their passivity because patience expresses the freedom and agency that only grace can sustain. Activity for God and passivity before God, doing and suffering, agency and patience, are two sides of the single coin of Christian discipleship. From their mutuality and balance comes contentment. So it is a grave error to exalt doing things at the expense of suffering things—or the opposite. The imitation of Christ requires that they always be held together:

> In active obedience we worship God by doing what pleases God, but by passive obedience we do as well worship God by being pleased with what God does. . . . It is but one side of a Christian to endeavor to do what pleases God; you must as well endeavor to be pleased with what God does.[17]

In Burroughs' eyes, patience is primarily the endurance of pain and loss with a tranquil and untroubled heart because even in the midst of desolation everything can be found again in a new way. Writing of riches, he comments, "It may be that while you had these things they shared with God in your affection, a great part of the stream of your affection ran that way; God would have the full stream run to him now." This involves not only the restoration of all that was lost but far more. Patience brings greater wealth than worldly activity could ever amass, for it unites us with the source of all richness. "This is the mystery of contentment. It makes up all its wants in God." The church on earth can pay homage to the glory and grandeur of God in a way that surpasses anything the church in heaven can offer, Burroughs writes, because "there is no work which God has made—the sun, moon, stars and all the world—in which so much of the glory of God appears as in a man who lives quietly in the midst of adversity." Saints and martyrs cannot bless and praise him in ways that match the devotions of the homeless, the handicapped, the hungry, and the afflicted. Therefore, we should rest content with our condition and not yearn too much for heaven, for right now we can serve God and proclaim his glory as all the angels in paradise are unable to do. The silence of the patient sufferer, in loneliness and confusion and loss, can resound more beautifully than all the music of the choirs of heaven. What need have they of patience? There are no temptations in heaven to overcome, and no afflictions as there are here on earth. Thus, Burroughs writes,

> Is it so much for one who is in Heaven... to be praising and blessing God, as for the poor soul who is in the midst of trials and temptations and afflictions and troubles? For this soul

> to go on praying, and blessing, and serving God, I say, is an excellence that you do not find in Heaven.[18]

The antithesis of Christian contentment is the impatience that desires to have its own way, and the punishment for such a terrible sin is that the impatient receive precisely what they think they want. The discontent that impatience breeds greatly aggravates our troubles, making even the least of them onerous burdens, because our attention remains fixed upon our pain or loss or the apparent injustices we have suffered until we can see nothing else and become the victims of obsession. Discontent is far from a minor sin; it stands in relation to Christianity as pride to humility, impatience to patience, selfishness to forgetfulness of the self, love of the world to love of God. Such impatience with the ways that providence has ordered human affairs is a challenge to God's goodness or sovereignty or wisdom, or an attack on all of them together, and therefore within it there is something truly satanic.

Like Satan himself, the phenomena of discontent are legion: envy and anger, boredom and sloth, sadness and despair, turbulence of spirit and resentment, greed and many more, all of which are expressed in the sin of murmuring, the rejection of the quiet of the contented heart. As circumstances vary, so can murmuring assume a thousand faces. It sees in every riddle of inequality a personal affront, impatient that it is not awarded preference over all others, persuaded that it knows better than God what justice requires, so quick to see the faults in its neighbors and so reluctant to recognize its own. Nowhere in the world is there anything about which it is not possible to complain. This is precisely the problem with it: murmuring expresses continuing engagement with the world instead of disengagement from it for Christ's sake; it is incapable of dying away from the world.

No matter how various its forms, however, they all display the same lack of humility, patience, and above all else, thankfulness. The penalty that such ingratitude reaps is a great constriction of our vision, and therefore the impoverishment of all our choices and opportunities, leading to a radically diminished sense of the wonders and the beauty of life. So it is scarcely surprising that "Scripture ranks unthankfulness among very great sins." In contrast, for the disciple gratitude is the chief motivation. How could one not respond with constant thankfulness to the love displayed at Calvary? How could patience, which finds its paradigm in the sufferings of Christ, ever lose its linkage to gratitude? Patience always has reason to be thankful. Burroughs counsels us not to concentrate upon current afflictions but to see them in the context of all God's past and present blessings, to practice patience in the knowledge that suffering is as important a part of discipleship as activity, and to endure adversity calmly: "Who am I, therefore, that the sun should always shine upon me, that I must have fair weather all my days?"[19]

One feature of Burroughs' thought that we have already seen in Calvin deserves special attention: the importance of vocation, or placement. He emphasizes its significance because of the perspective upon suffering pain or loss that is afforded by the sense of being in the right place:

> Be sure of your call to every business you go about. . . . Then, whatever you meet with, you may quiet your heart with this: I know I am where God would have me. Nothing in the world will quiet the heart so much as this: when I meet with any cross, I know I am where God would have me, in my place and calling.[20]

Placement is simply one element within a Christian doctrine of providence, but this explicit treatment of it even more strongly

reinforces the patience and calling of the disciple to be a Christ to his or her neighbor, in God's own time and at the place that God has set. It is sometimes assumed that the idea is peculiarly Lutheran, because of the way that Luther extended the medieval notion of vocation or *beruf* to include not only churchly callings but also secular employment and relationships. In fact, however, it is equally well anchored in the Reformed tradition.

Perhaps *The Rare Jewel of Christian Contentment* was so popular in the seventeenth century because patience, for many reasons, was a central concern in Puritan reflection and piety. Burroughs' work is an extraordinary combination of doctrinalism and empiricism, rigorous Calvinist theology on the one hand and a wealth of psychological detail on the other. At first there seems something rather arbitrary and contrived in his scheme, in which he lays out thirteen excuses of a discontented heart, fifteen mysteries of contentment and ten excellences of it, thirteen evils of a murmuring spirit, ten considerations to content the heart in affliction, and so forth. But the truth is that Burroughs' work is a classic, an impressive union of imaginative exploration and simple common sense in which theological wisdom and ordinary experience are related to one another in ways that testify persuasively to the "empirical fit" of Christian faith.

These themes of contentment and murmuring may seem old wine poured into new semantic bottles to conserve the distinctive accents of Puritanism. But changes of vocabulary can be useful to illustrate the continuing relevance of very old traditions and their enduring power to expose the labyrinthine ways of the heart. Burroughs contributes to our understanding of patience in several ways. One is his extended emphasis upon action and passion as equally important and inseparable sides of discipleship, while another is his belief that patient suffering

gives greater praise to God than the saints can offer in paradise. Still another is the way he explores the relationship between patience and gratitude. Thankfulness is more than sufficient reason for us to be patient, not only in our relationship with God but in all human affairs.

During the two hundred years after Jeremiah Burroughs' death, there was certainly no lack of Christian studies of the importance of patience. Many of their authors, both Catholic and Protestant, had their own special vocabularies, accents, and emphases. But it was not until the middle of the nineteenth century that Søren Kierkegaard's *Purity of Heart* appeared, a book so unprecedented and uncompromising in its portrayal of what religious patience demands that it added a new chapter to the history of the virtue precisely when patience had been widely discounted by the social reformers of the day. Although he had once contemplated an ecclesiastical vocation, Kierkegaard became instead the impassioned critic of the Lutheran church in Denmark, a "gadfly" denouncing the "double-mindedness" of an institution that saw no conflict in serving both God and mammon. Yet Kierkegaard was also in debt to this church. His prolific writings were always indelibly shaped by his Lutheran heritage, both his academic works and the essays devoted to the nurture of the congregations of Copenhagen.

The Danish word that we translate as patience, *taalmod,* does not appear with great frequency in the pseudonymous writings of Kierkegaard that have so profoundly influenced modern theology and ethics, but its various meanings serve as a counterpoint to his dominant motifs. In the writings that were published under his own name, however, what is implied

elsewhere becomes the center of attention. These several dozen "edifying discourses" were written for the upbuilding of the faithful, not so much to clarify Christian claims as to confirm Christian souls. In the discourses patience is a dominant refrain, and nowhere more so than in *Purity of Heart.*

This invitation to Christian self-examination begins and ends with the same prayer, asking for the ability to will one thing only: "In prosperity may Thou grant perseverance to will one thing; amid distractions, collectedness to will one thing; in suffering, patience to will one thing." Perseverance, collectedness, and patience as expressions of purity of heart are worlds apart from the four sorts of "double-mindedness" that afflict the half-hearted Christian, who desires what is good for the sake of reward or out of fear of punishment, as a form of self-assertion, or as one option out of many. The last of these is the most common: people treat the good as though it were only one choice among many, for they are unwilling to abandon the more ordinary goods of family and friends and wealth and reputation. But such attachments mean they have lost their genuine good entirely. Double-mindedness is always an attempt to have God, or "the Good," without relinquishing the world and its comforts. Such attempts to yoke Christ and Caesar are always hypocritical and fruitless. Loving what is good out of a desire for reward or a fear of punishment are two sides of the same coin; if we love in order to avoid punishment, then we refuse the one medicine that can restore us to health. If we were pure of heart, Kierkegaard argues, we would fear not punishment but wrongdoing. If we do something that is wrong, then we should not fear the punishment that might heal us "just as medicine heals the sick."[21] If we fear the medicine, then what we really fear is health. The patience to will one thing in the midst of suffering is a crucial ingredient in the Christian life; chastisement is the only medicine that can restore wholeness to the fractured self.

In Kierkegaard's explorations of double-mindedness, his most subtle and important comments on patience occur in the portrayal of those who love the Good as a form of self-assertion, those who are "active early and late 'for the sake of the Good,' storming about noisily and restlessly." Such apparent heroism, however, is ultimately self-centered and impatient. Christian athleticism means that a person

> cannot, he will not, understand the Good's slowness; that out of mercy the Good is slow; that out of love for free persons, it will not use force; that in its wisdom toward the frail ones, it shrinks from any deception. He cannot, he will not, humbly understand that the Good can get on without him.[22]

The divine mercy means that "the Good is slow"—these are memorable words, indeed. The divine power means that God himself could assume the form of a servant and become obedient even to death. The divine richness signifies that God is not diminished by the poverty of clothing himself in time, or accepting the limitations of flesh. "The Good puts on the slowness of time as a poor garment, and in keeping with this change of dress one who serves it must be clothed in the insignificant figure of the unprofitable servant."[23] The victories of God are from everlasting to everlasting. Our heroic attempts to anticipate or replicate them in time express an impatience that understands nothing of God's patient ways. Ultimately it is selfish, no better and perhaps even worse than other forms of double-mindedness.

Those who truly will the Good must be willing to suffer all as well as do all for it. Here Kierkegaard's focus is upon the suffering that is useless by worldly standards and a burden to everyone it touches, yet to which the sufferer has agreed for the sake of the Good. Strength is made perfect in weakness by

patience, which is not mere surrender to the inevitable but rather a victory over circumstances. It becomes the foundation upon which we achieve our highest end, purity of heart. For the sake of the Good, then, we can accept punishment as a medicine for sin, agree even to apparently senseless suffering, and win a victory unknown to those whose health and happiness have never been in question. "Never forget," Kierkegaard admonishes us, "that the devout wise man wishes no stroke of adversity to be taken away when it comes his way, because he cannot know whether or not it may be good for him."[24]

Patience can perform even greater feats than courage, breathing freedom into an otherwise lifeless world. Courage, Kierkegaard writes, chooses the suffering that could otherwise be avoided, whereas patience wins its freedom in unavoidable suffering. It makes a virtue of necessity, so to speak, because the assent it expresses "brings a determination of freedom out of that which is determined as necessity." The Danish word for courage is *mod,* which is contained within the word for patience, *taalmod.* Patience may sometimes be a particular form of fortitude, but it is also the bearer and sustainer of courage when the nights are long and dark, and it can foster a new and inalienable liberty when courage has lost the freedom it first possessed.

Kierkegaard stands on its head the view of Thomas Aquinas that patience is a mere derivative of the higher virtue of fortitude. This reversal of their relationship is an extraordinary statement in the middle of a century that tended to exaggerate the possibilities of courage but dismissed the importance of patience, and it is also a helpful corrective to inflexible distinctions between greater and lesser virtues. Patience is not resignation, passivity, or inaction; rather, it is the emergence of freedom within the domain where necessity rules. Patience

affirms that there is no realm, no matter how inhospitable and frightening, that cannot be visited by God's grace. To the eyes of faith, these victories of the personal in the arena of chance and fate testify that, even where necessity rules, the world belongs to God.

Kierkegaard knows as well as Augustine and countless others that the patience of which he writes is not a human achievement but a gift from God. But his emphasis lies upon our personal appropriation of that grace, so that we may wholeheartedly enter into the commitment that God has enabled us to undertake. In every way, *Purity of Heart* is truly an exercise in self-examination. What renders Kierkegaard's treatment of patience so distinctive and important is that its imperatives seem exceedingly harsh: namely, the desire for punishment and the willing of pain that is utterly meaningless by the standards of this world. That is why the double-mindedness of the faint-hearted Christian seems all the more plausible. No other great theologian has distinguished so sharply and relentlessly as Kierkegaard between the demands of Christian patience and its secular counterpart, without which all human courtesy dissolves. But there is nothing masochistic in *Purity of Heart*. It is simply an attempt to delineate without compromise the meaning of single-mindedness in relation to God and therefore what Christian patience must entail.

To say that purity of heart means both doing and suffering for the Good brings Kierkegaard to an important discussion of means and ends. He insists that patience is as fundamental to the exercise of our agency as it is to our suffering, because the end never justifies the means. If means were not as important as ends, the self could not will one thing in a single-minded way. "Eternally speaking, there is only one means and there is only one end: the means and the end are one and the same thing." Therefore, if we set goals for ourselves and fail to reach them,

we may still be found blameless and even praiseworthy if our failure stems from our reluctance to employ means that are unworthy of our commitment to the Good. Precisely because eternity is not impatient, we must be always patient in the choice of our means; we will be eternally responsible for the means we choose. When we use only those means that are genuinely good, then, in the eyes of eternity, we have reached the goal.[25] If the reward is great, so also is the price. When we practice such patience, we will in "the slowness of time" appear, not only in others' eyes but in ours as well, unprofitable servants. Deeply inscribed in us is a passion to return to the sovereign Giver with some small gift, in humble recognition of all God has done. Gratitude becomes an uncontrollable itch if it can find no way at all to express itself. But if our means are unworthy of our ends, our gratitude is no more than egotism, double-mindedness.

At the farthest imaginable remove from the person who does all for the Good there is the extraordinary person who is endowed with a multitude of talents and indefatigable energy, whose interests are boundless and whose good works are legion. And yet, Kierkegaard warns, this busyness is a deadly disease, for it is never free from the taint of self-love. It cannot and will not understand that the best we can do is to meet God with empty hands; instead of busyness, there must be surrender. Busyness means distraction, while surrender means collectedness—the single-minded focus upon the one thing necessary. The trouble with busyness is that it affords no leisure to pause, to stop everything. If we cannot pause, how can we listen to anything above the noise of the crowd? How can we see anything when the landscape is so rapidly changing? Or how can we touch anyone when all are so quickly carried away? "Pausing is not a sluggish repose," Kierkegaard notes. "Pausing is also movement. It is the inward movement of the heart. To

pause is to deepen oneself in inwardness. But merely going further is to go straight in the direction of superficiality."[26] The remedy is patience, which pauses until it can decipher someone else's words or examine some strange scene or touch a neighbor's heart by a gesture of support. Sometimes patience is not rewarded with what it expects or wants, but even so, the way it clarifies our vision is the foundation for everything else, the "best of all." Without patience, we have no self-examination; without self-examination, we have no guideposts along the road to single-mindedness, to purity of heart.

During 1843 and 1844, Kierkegaard published eighteen edifying discourses under his own name, of which four deal directly with patience. The first is a meditation on Job and on the words "The Lord gave, and the Lord took away; blessed be the name of the Lord." In the terrible moment when the Lord took away all his children, Job

> did not first say, "The Lord took away," but first of all he said, "The Lord gave."...The first thing the loss of everything did was to make him thankful to the Lord that he had given him all the blessings that he now took away from him.[27]

Nothing can diminish the proportions of Job's loss, but there is still reason for him to give thanks for what he once had; the pain of deprivation illuminates how rich these blessings were. It is not true that memories of happy times diminish our loss, but they can prevent the loss from blotting out everything else and thus bringing us to despair.

There are people who blame their wretchedness and deprivation on the evil that others do, or on chance, or on the forces of nature. They say, "It was not the Lord who has taken it away; it was an accident." Yet this attempt to preserve faith in

God is ultimately devastating, for it acknowledges God's presence and power only in times of good fortune and blessing. Job, however,

> traced everything back to God. . . . The very moment everything was taken away from him, he knew it was the Lord who had taken it away, and therefore in his loss he. . . maintained intimacy with the Lord; he saw the Lord, and therefore he did not see despair.

The house of Job will always remain a place of sorrow. Because he is able to bless the Lord despite all his deprivations, however, he affirms that he is not alone and is not forever the prisoner of his pain. Therefore, in the end God has not divested him of all that he possessed:

> Job collected all his sorrow, as it were, and "cast it upon the Lord," and then the Lord took that away from him also, and only praise was left and in it his heart's incorruptible joy.[28]

Patience has reason to be grateful even in the midst of turmoil and suffering, and so it affords a perspective without which faith simply cannot endure. This is the greatest of the works of patience, to say everywhere and always, "Blessed be the name of the Lord." The scholar D. Z. Phillips writes: "Patience in religion takes the form of the ability to thank, to find things worthwhile, despite the way things go."[29] This definition of patience as the ability to thank is as profound and illuminating as it is unusual—we will not find it in a dictionary. But if thanksgiving is not among the conventional definitions of patience, one might still argue that it underlies and inspires and sustains every virtue. Certainly giving thanks should be a major theme in any Christian interpretation of patience. On this point as on so many others, Kierkegaard has much to teach, as did Jeremiah Burroughs two centuries before him, and most especially to a culture like ours, where the moment is all.

In another brief discourse on patience, Kierkegaard writes that it is not only a necessary condition for gaining the soul but is itself the meaning of possessing it. Patience is not only the single-minded pursuit of the Good but a manifestation of living from it and in unbroken unity with it. The means and the end are no different at all.

> If the person who wants to gain his soul does not want to understand that when he has won patience he has won what he needed, what was of more value than any other winning, then he will never gain it. . . . The condition, therefore, after it has served the gaining, remains as that which is gained.[30]

Few have written more brilliantly of Christian patience than Søren Kierkegaard, and certainly no one has ever articulated more rigorously the magnitude of its demands. For Kierkegaard the greatest work of religious patience is the readiness to thank, everywhere and always. Patience is an act of freedom that softens "the iron realm of necessity," and in this lies its superiority to courage. Patience is the work of single-mindedness: the eye of the mind is concentrated on one thing alone, in contrast to the distracted busyness that is incapable of pausing in order to see the world as it is and not only as we would have it be. In willing to do all as well as suffer all for the sake of the Good, patience teaches us to proceed slowly. If means are not perfectly suited to ends we will sink back into double-mindedness again. No brief summary can begin to convey the richness of Kierkegaard's work, but it can suggest the distinctive accents that he adds to the contributions of Calvin and Burroughs toward a fuller understanding of what Christian patience means.

Chapter Six

Patience Defined

endurance, forbearance, expectancy, and perseverance

It is a strange coincidence that in the middle of this century three literary works, published to great public acclaim, addressed the same topic in the course of three or four years. Their common focus is the theme of endless waiting and unrewarded patience in a senseless world, and in this they are very much a product of the intellectual climate of the postwar world and the philosophy of existentialism. The first is Samuel Beckett's play *Waiting for Godot*, which is a wonderful parody of patience in which two tramps, Estragon and Vladimir, sit under a tree on a country road waiting for a mysterious figure, Godot, who may or may not be coming to meet them. Neither is sure, and at the end of the play they are still waiting. The second is Archibald MacLeish's retelling of the book of Job, *J. B.* In contrast to the biblical story, however, the counsel that Job eventually accepts comes not from God but from the modest humanism of Sarah, his wife:

> The candles in churches are out.
> The lights have gone out in the sky.
> Blow on the coal of the heart
> And we'll see, by and by.[1]

Even if we can make no sense of the world or worship at the altars built by earlier generations, there is still "the coal of the heart," reason enough for us to cultivate habits of forbearance, endurance, loyalty, pity, and compassion.

It is the third of these works that deserves our particular attention. Albert Camus' essay *The Myth of Sisyphus* also portrays a world without God, but one in which a certain form of patience is the foundation for a distinctively human protest against a meaningless existence. Some nameless crime has condemned Sisyphus to push a great rock to the top of a mountain only to see it fall back to the bottom of its own weight. He is condemned to do this without respite forever; his life is the unvarying repetition of this futile labor. So patience is Sisyphus' calling. His perseverance constantly renews the consciousness that can protest against his fate, and so he leaves some sort of human mark upon the world. Without patience, the crimes of the world go unchallenged and unnoticed. Unlike the worlds of Beckett and MacLeish, then, this is a universe in which patience not only avails, it prevails—in a sense. Patience creates enduring meaning where otherwise there would be no meaning whatsoever.

If we compare Camus' version of patience with that of an ancient philosophical tradition that we have already encountered in our discussion of Tertullian, we have a notable illustration of the ways that words can change their meanings and even reverse themselves when they are enlisted for different purposes. On the one hand, we have the patience of Sisyphus in the face of a meaningless world; on the other, there

is the patience of the Stoic wise man, who has found the strength to detach himself from the world and especially the life of the passions. His heroic self-sufficiency is equally indifferent to all the torments that the world can inflict and to the joys it so fleetingly offers. Thus we have two ways utterly opposed, two different worlds in which the nature and role of patience are entirely at odds. Of course neither the example of Sisyphus nor the Stoic can instruct us directly in what patience has meant within the Christian tradition. What they can do, however, is reveal the central importance of the virtue in two diametrically opposed views of the world, one secular and the other religious, and illustrate some of the very different ways in which patience itself can be understood. Patience is a crucial motif for both, and yet in each it conveys assumptions and expectations that conflict with one another beyond any hope of reconciliation. There is no way to bring them together, this protest in the name of human passion and submissive passionlessness, even though they both bear the name of patience.

The consenting sage and the protesting Sisyphus live close by one another. Their likenesses are as profound as their great dissimilarities. Both are solitary heroes who, were they ever to meet anyone else at all, would meet only themselves again. For different reasons, their landscapes will not sustain any sort of diversity. Neither can ever know the joy of an encounter with someone different, genuinely other, that requires the exercise of forms of patience they have never known. They are also one in their individualism. If there is a tenuous impulse toward the companionship of like with like in Stoicism, there is still no real dialogue or interdependence there, no sense that the fundamental units of human existence are not individuals in their solitude, but persons in relationship. They are one as well in the constriction of their vision. Neither can imagine anything beyond the endless duration of present circumstances. They have been

granted no intimation that another sort of patience could dream of more than this, that it can see beyond the moment if imagination is sufficiently provisioned and firmly anchored in the richness and expansiveness of the real world. These are the two great differences that bind together Sisyphus and the sage, despite all that separates them: individualism and a failure of imagination.

Sisyphus endures for the sake of his complaint. He must persevere. Patience is always preferable to suicide because of the small victory that consciousness affords. But his sight is bounded by the dimensions of his stone. Vision can encompass no possibilities not yet realized. Life is repetition, never other, never more. Suffering is all. The sage also inhabits a world where there will never be anything new. It is a divine and therefore determined universe that testifies to no values beyond itself, allows no room for dreams, admits no unrealized possibilities, offers no genuine futurity. In its different way this is a universe that limits the range of vision no less severely than Sisyphus' rock. In neither world is there anything malleable, anything amenable to a sculptor's tools, talent, or imagination. In neither is there anything that might legitimate another version of patience—one that could offer a lengthened perspective or allow a spontaneous gesture, the free play of the imagination, true expectancy.

Despite all the continuities we have seen in the Christian tradition, patience has been very differently perceived in the course of many centuries and in diverse cultures. On the one hand, the preceding chapters certainly suggest that at least until our own time, there has been real consensus about the meanings of patience and its radical importance for the life of

the believer. On the other, we have also encountered different shades of meaning attached to the idea of patience—many different accents and emphases and a great welter of connotations as rich as they are diverse. Now it is time to marshall the witness of all these Christian writers. We must sort and sift through the skein of meanings we have encountered in order to determine more precisely how Christian patience should be understood.

Let us explore four definitions of patience, all from the *Oxford English Dictionary*, for together they reflect the fundamentals of what we have learned from scripture and in the church's tradition.[2] First, patience is "the suffering or enduring (of pain, trouble, or evil) with calmness and composure; the quality or capacity of so suffering or enduring." Unfortunately, it is a common error to identify patience entirely with the quiet endurance of adversity, and perhaps this was a significant reason for the eclipse of the virtue in the nineteenth century, when social transformation became the great ambition of Christians and secularists alike. Suffering with contentment or tranquillity is a better definition than mere stolid endurance, because it reminds us that the fundamental unit of human life is not a single person but persons in relation. Life is responsiveness. We suffer far more than adversity: we constantly "suffer" the caring and admonitions of our parents, the encouragements, remonstrances, and challenges of our friends and colleagues, the discipline and instruction of our teachers. It is only as we patiently bear all this that we are furnished with the resources that maturity requires. Suffering the concern that others have for us can bring us the strength that adversity demands.

The second definition is "forbearance, long-suffering, longanimity under provocation of any kind; especially forbearance or bearing with others, their faults, limitations," as

in Shakespeare's reference to "an old abusing of Gods patience." Forbearance means tolerance of the differences among us and sympathy with the weaknesses of others, such as when we choose to ignore unkind words spoken in a moment of anger. It certainly does not ever mean condoning any sort of crime or violation, for that would mean we have abandoned the culprit and been indifferent to the threats these actions pose for our life together.

Third, patience is "the calm abiding of the issue of time, processes...quiet and self-possessed waiting for something: 'the quality of expecting long without rage or discontent.'" In everyday speech this is what patience often describes, but contemporary assumptions render it perhaps the most elusive form of the virtue. If the moment is all, we cannot afford to settle for less than instant gratification. So a willingness to wait must not be confused with a lack of purpose, either tentativeness or indecision. On the contrary, this form of patience can often be the mother of invention because it forces us to pause and examine our surroundings with new appreciation.

Finally, patience can mean "constancy in labor, exertion, or effort." Like suffering or endurance, perseverance has to do not only with recalcitrant or adversarial situations. Such persistence can also describe the constancy and fidelity of a scholar devoted to her research, an artist to his painting, an architect to his drawings, or a mother to teaching her child some new skill.

Let us accept these four as the primary meanings of patience: calm *endurance,* or suffering without discontent; *forbearance* or tolerance, bearing with the faults and frailties of others with equanimity; *willingness to wait* without resentment, or calm expectancy on the threshold of tomorrow; and *perseverance* without surrender, unwearying constancy and

consistency. From a Christian perspective it is wrong to think of these as four sorts of patience, one or two of which can be cultivated apart from the others. Faith insists that all four are mutually reinforcing and finally inseparable. This is another significant difference between the Christian tradition and the kinds of patience that Camus and Stoicism offer us.

The idea of patience can be approached from three different perspectives, and it is useful to distinguish them. First, it is an essential motif in the Christian tradition and its scriptures, where it is upheld as one of the perfections of God and an important theological virtue that we can acquire by grace alone. Second, patience is one of the virtues that must be developed by anyone who aspires to moral selfhood, quite apart from religious commitment. Third, it is a "civic virtue," so to speak, essential for the stability of society. The relationship between genuinely moral and merely civic is not unlike the distinction between reality and appearance. Patience "writ small" means common courtesy, consideration, politeness, the basic civility that our common life requires—such as the willingness of drivers to treat pedestrians and cyclists as equal members of the human race. Such civility is far from the heroism that may be demanded for the endurance of terrible affliction. It does, however, have its own modest elements of endurance, forbearance, perseverance, and the willingness to wait companionably. Without them there is simply no reason to believe that we can survive our life together. We must cherish them if we cherish ourselves.

The idea of patience is much the richest when it is understood as a theological virtue and not simply as a moral achievement. Only biblical and historical studies can capture the wealth of connotations and resonances that patience acquires in a Christian perspective, or clothe with enough density and detail the thinness of dictionary definitions. So let

us return to the theologians we discussed earlier in order to summarize at least some of the motifs that are essential elements in a comprehensive account of patience as a Christian virtue.

For Tertullian, patience is the highest virtue because it is really a synonym for the obedience of the Son of God and inseparable from the humility Christ has taught us to emulate. In contrast, impatience is our original sin, the motive for Satan's temptation of Adam and Eve and the reason for their fall. It is an ingredient in every sin whatsoever. This is one of Tertullian's distinctive accents: patience must be cultivated because impatience is the root of every sin. Another is the way that he yokes patience and asceticism: we must patiently surrender some of the world's goods we might easily have for ourselves when other people are threatened by famine and disease. Cyprian echoes Tertullian's comments about patience as one of God's perfections that is supremely revealed in Jesus Christ. Indeed, Cyprian is convinced that patience affords a principle of interpretation for all of the scriptures. Perhaps what is most characteristic, however, is the emphasis of this extraordinary pastor on the church as a patient community, practicing forbearance toward all in the midst of an impatient world always intent upon a rush to judgment.

Augustine builds upon the foundations laid by Tertullian and Cyprian and particularly stresses the interdependence of patience, humility, and gratitude. But he emphasizes more systematically and with more exegetical sophistication that Christian patience is wholly the work of God, a gift of grace that is utterly unlike the patience that sinners display. His special focus is upon patience in the form of perseverance, the hope for which is the sum and substance of the Lord's Prayer. Gregory is the first writer to comment extensively on the patience of Job, whose uncomplaining endurance despite the loss of everything

prefigures the way of the Christ and the vocation of the church. He understands patience as "the root and guardian" of all the virtues because it has to do not with a cheerful countenance so much as with the orientation of the heart, the contentment and peace that the world cannot give. But his distinctive emphasis is the fruit of his meditation on Job's patience, the tranquil endurance of loss in order that one might not oneself be lost to God.

Perhaps what is most striking in Thomas Aquinas, in comparison with those who wrote before him, is his definition of virtue, based on Aristotle, as a mean between the extremes of excess and defect. So patience, which is the uncomplaining endurance of adversity, is a mean between impatience and indifference, or apathy. It is a kind of courage that sustains us in this life, while courage itself is reserved for the prospect of death. In Thomas à Kempis, patience involves discipleship, companionship with the risen Christ and with the whole company of the faithful; without patience there can be no mutuality and companionship. In the passion and death of Christ, no graces except love are more apparent than quiet endurance and unfailing forbearance. So Christian patience, united with humility, is the very soul of our vocation to live in imitation of Christ. His characteristic emphasis lies on companionship as the secret of life and the patience it always requires. Another distinctive feature in Thomas à Kempis is the patience that we must show to ourselves.

Perhaps no one has ever insisted more strenuously than John Calvin that patience is primarily an expression of confidence in the providence of God. Whatever is visited upon us is intended by a gracious Lord to bring us ultimately into fellowship with himself. Endurance and perseverance are the principal forms of the virtue, but not its only ones. Calvin strongly emphasizes the power of patience to transform every

imaginable situation. Patience lies at the center of both self-denial and bearing the cross, which are the conditions of discipleship. It is always an acknowledgment that, wherever we are, we have been placed there by the will of God; this is one of his more distinctive themes.

In the work of the remarkable Puritan divine Jeremiah Burroughs, patience signifies contentment with the providence of God, thankfulness for it, and the readiness to keep silent before the Lord. Patience has nothing in common with mere resignation, which is far from thankful: it has to do with human initiative and inventiveness. Its opposite is murmuring, which is an expression of ingratitude and a failure to acknowledge that God has placed us where we are. Patience, humility, and gratitude together help the disciple endure whatever the world inflicts.

Finally, Søren Kierkegaard emphasizes a sense in which patience is a virtue superior to courage, for it can bring an element of freedom into what is otherwise the impersonal realm of necessity. Patience knows that the meaning of discipleship is suffering, which involves not merely endurance but the recognition that God alone can perform the will of God. One distinctive note is Kierkegaard's insight that patience realizes the profound limitations placed upon the means that can be used to achieve even the highest ends. The Christian is warned not to anticipate the divine will or strive to bring in the kingdom of God by human effort. Consequently, patience is the antidote for the distraction and busyness that characterize the modern world. It describes the capacity to pause and to give thanks. Christian patience is always thankful; this is another distinctive motif, as it was in Jeremiah Burroughs.

In the work of so many of these writers, the three virtues of patience, humility, and gratitude are constantly linked. They are no less inseparable and no less theological than are faith and hope and love, and no farther from the center of the Christian life. Each carries its two companions within itself, so that when one is discovered all are found, and where one is absent none will long endure. Even though this summary is far from complete, surely it is persuasive testimony that Christian patience is one of the greatest resources for our avowal of faith in God and for the protection of our own humanity. From the root of the word for patience have sprung many of the hardy perennials of our language: not only compassion, compatible, passion, and passive, but also penance, penitence, pain, and similar cognates too numerous to list. It is scarcely cause for surprise, therefore, that this virtue, which seems at first so small and commonplace, becomes a window through which we encounter the greatest themes of the Christian vision and the abiding issues that continue to excite and torment the human spirit—suffering and sacrifice, punishment and expiation, reconciliation and love, creativity and fulfillment.

Within the confines of a single paragraph let us now attempt to tie together what has been said so far and offer a definition of patience as a theological virtue. Patience is a gift of grace that makes possible the imitation of Jesus Christ, in whose life and death this perfection of God's own nature is fully disclosed. It confronts whatever it suffers, secure in the knowledge that human life is mutuality ruled by divine love and that it has been placed where it is by the hand of God. Patience is the chief exercise of love; without it, no love or companionship is Christian. It is united with humility and gratitude; the three can be distinguished but never separated. Christian patience is always thankful. As an act that expresses our freedom from the world as well as our openness to it, patience blesses the Creator

of that freedom. In our relationships with others it is a form of justice or fair play that seeks for them no less than what God's patience has granted to us, but it knows there are restrictions on the means it can employ in pursuit of that end. All these accents enrich its four fundamental meanings as disciplined endurance, undying expectancy, unselfish forbearance, and realistic perseverance. In contrast, impatience and ingratitude are at the center of our estrangement. So the idea of Christian patience really becomes a summary of the life of discipleship and the meaning of the imitation of Christ.

The theological foundations for the virtue are rich and various. Although patience is a persistent theme in the scriptures, we have seen that it is displayed more often by God's forbearance toward his errant creatures than in the fitful fidelity of the chosen people or even the disciples themselves toward their Lord. So patience is typically disclosed as a divine perfection rather than a human virtue, because God is true to himself in all that he does. Of all the names of God in the Bible, the most important is Father. All other titles and attributions must be interpreted in its light. God's might and creativity are simply qualifications of this unique fatherhood: the former means that God possesses the power to fulfill all his fatherly purposes, and the latter that all God's purposes are fatherly. So the definitive description of the self is that it is a child of God. At the heart and center of this relationship is God's patience, his lovingkindness and long-sufferingness and forbearance. The revelation of the divine name directs us to the human relationship of parent and child in order to best understand that patience is foundational in all human affairs.

Because God is Father, creation is grace. God does not begrudge the self plenty of room for the expression of its creaturely powers. God patiently stands a hand's breadth off, so to speak. His inexhaustible forbearance guards and sustains

even the errant creature. God wills what is utterly distinct and different from himself; as Luther wrote, he does so from "pure, fatherly, and divine goodness and mercy."[3] The Father is still at work in the world, patiently judging and transforming it to achieve his own design. For this reason, too, the virtue is at the core of discipleship. Christians are called to pause and look more deeply into things, so they can decipher and respond to the activity of God in their current affairs.

Finally, the Father is the one who promises to make all things new. Christianity is a thoroughly eschatological faith that believes God's patience cannot ultimately be thwarted. Therefore our human demands for patience find a counterpoint in the counsel of faith to look patiently beyond every tomorrow. St. Paul's eschatological imperative to live "as if" and "as if not"—as if this present age were not and as if God's new age had come in fullness and power—provides a foundation and focus for perseverance. He insists upon the opportunities that the present age affords while easing the burdens of endurance within it.

As a theological virtue, however, patience finds its ultimate inspiration in the story of Jesus Christ, as writers such as Tertullian and à Kempis and Calvin so forcefully insist; it is in the ministry of the Son that God discloses himself as the eternal Father and our father by adoption. In turning to Christology, W. H. Vanstone's *The Stature of Waiting* offers a particularly valuable perspective because of the way it knits together aspects of the biblical witness and some elements of our most frustrating and yet unavoidable experience. Vanstone certainly portrays Jesus as a model of patience, but his interests ultimately extend far beyond the virtue itself. He brings into theological focus the fundamental refrain of these chapters—the interdependent nature of our humanity and the

importance of suffering understood as reciprocity and mutuality.

In his interpretation of the passion narrative, Vanstone writes not only of patience as a virtue but of the dignity and potential of every self as a patient, a dependent, an object, because that status has been sanctified once for all by God's acceptance of it for himself. It is this claim, so much at odds with our assumptions today, that he believes must be a basic Christian affirmation in an age when so many people are less often independent actors than patients—or, in language he prefers, objects rather than subjects. This shift from the patience of the self to the self as a patient moves from Christology to a justification for the virtue that is written into the fundamentals of the human situation.

As Vanstone understands the passion story, Jesus not only suffers, he entirely surrenders his own initiative to the initiative of others. By his own free decision, he is no longer a subject but an object, no longer one actor among many but merely acted upon, purely a patient. The first chapters of *The Stature of Waiting* are a study of the rather neutral and colorless Greek verb *paradidomi,* which means "to hand over." It is significant in the New Testament because it is the word used to describe what happens to Jesus in the garden of Gethsemane, what is done to him by the Jewish leaders before Pilate, and what Pilate himself does at the end of the trial of Jesus. Vanstone asks why the writers of the gospels assigned such importance to the story of Jesus' betrayal by Judas, when the course of events had already been set in motion. Its prominence is not merely a recognition of what is needed for a powerful and compelling narrative, but a decisive expression of "the conviction of the earliest Christian believers that, whatever else was said about Jesus, it must be said that He was handed over." If the deed's historical importance is slight, its symbolic and theological significance is

immense. We know from St. Paul's writings that before the gospels appeared,

> when Christians wanted to say what it was, in all that they knew about Jesus, that mattered most and was most important to them, they said that "He was handed over...for our sake."...Any incident in the narrative, such as Pilate's verdict, which could be represented as a "handing over" of Jesus would be so represented; and the shameful but historically unimportant deed of Judas would provide a particularly important niche.[4]

Vanstone's study of "handing over" seeks to show that in some sense there is complete discontinuity between the ministry of Jesus and his passion, when he was no longer the agent whose sovereign freedom and initiative could not be evaded but entirely a sufferer, purely the recipient of the deeds of others. Although he is the subject of the whole New Testament narrative, he is an actor only in its first part. The passion does not mean only that he endured the cruelty of those he came to save and died upon a cross, but that he who had been the master was completely mastered by others, he who had been the architect of events became their pawn:

> He was handed over to wait upon and receive the decisions and deeds of men, to become an object in their hands....He passes from doing to receiving what others do, from working to waiting, from the role of subject to that of object and, in the proper sense of the phrase, from action to passion.[5]

Yet this passivity was not enforced but chosen, and it was certainly as essential to Jesus' redemptive mission as all the teachings and mighty works that had preceded it. The activity and passivity, agency and passion, initiative and awaiting are entirely distinct, but they are also united as the twin acts of his

freedom. The power of God, partly disclosed in his mighty acts, is fully revealed when Jesus allows himself to be handed over:

> It is that transition itself, that willed exchange of impassibility for passion, which decisively discloses His divinity—the glory of God in Him. . . . Jesus destines Himself, by His own will, to wait upon the decisions and deeds of men; He works, one might say, towards a climax in which He must wait. . . . One might say that the ultimate glory of God's creativity is the creation of His own exposure to that which He has created: that of all that God has done in and for the world the most glorious thing is this—that He has handed Himself over to the world.[6]

Certainly the redemptive significance of the passion of Jesus is bound up with his whole life of obedience to the Father. Yet the ultimate instance of his power is the relinquishing of power, the consummate expression of his activity is his patience, and the greatest use of his initiative lies in waiting and endurance. So the obedience of the Son to the Father culminates in his submission to the hands of men, when the world's redemption is achieved. Vanstone wants to isolate this claim and highlight it in all its mysteriousness, so that we might learn more of the meaning of our humanity and submit our own preconceptions and assumptions to the corrective of the biblical narrative. In Jesus Christ, God affirms and sanctifies the existence of the self, both as subject and as object, but it is above all in the latter that his glory is disclosed.

It is true that the waiting and suffering that Jesus experienced were freely chosen, affirmed by him in obedience to the Father. Yet much of the passivity, vulnerability, and erosion of initiative that are our ordinary lot are forced upon us by powers beyond our control, with consequences that we would never have chosen for ourselves. Nevertheless, it is

absolutely essential for us to affirm this dependence, helplessness, and need to wait upon the initiatives of others, for these have all been sanctified by God in Jesus Christ. They are not impoverishments of our nature, but the inevitabilities of our life together. They do not compromise our dignity, but can, in fact, greatly enhance it. They do not represent an inferior condition and it is mistaken, even malicious, to judge them so. Furthermore, often our waiting is freely embraced; then, at least on occasion, "waiting can be the most intense and poignant of all human experiences—the experience which, above all others, strips us of affectation and self-deception and reveals to us the reality of our needs, our values and ourselves."[7]

We learn the importance of waiting and patience especially in our love of others. Unless parents show patience to their children and wait for them to progress at their own speed, they shall have deprived their children of the room that is their birthright as the children of God. Children must be patient with parents, too, for even when their sight and mind and limbs have become less acute and supple, they can still love with all the strength and ferocity of youth. Love consigns us to vulnerability, suffering, waiting, and a certain passivity:

> By our activity of loving we destine ourselves...to waiting—to placing in the hands of another the outcome of our own endeavor....Through our own initiative in loving, we create a situation of which the issue passes out of our hands.[8]

Despite his deep conviction of the mutuality and reciprocity, the dependence and interdependence of human life, Vanstone does not offer us an extensive analysis of selfhood, although a dialogical or relational model of the person seems to leap from every page. Instead, he simply insists that as we become more enmeshed in the systems that our own

technological wizardry has devised, we will experience a freedom that was previously unimaginable. Despite this, we will also come to experience ourselves as passive rather than active, as the possessed instead of the possessors, as objects as often as subjects. These themes resound with all the force of a litany throughout his work. In the world that he envisions, it will be true

> that one's daily bread should be provided rather than earned or achieved: that one should receive by gift rather than acquire by right: that one should lose one's independence: that one should wait upon the world rather than work upon it.[9]

Even though all these possibilities run counter to prevailing attitudes and expectations, they need not diminish the dignity and status of those who will dwell in the land of tomorrow. There, too, it will be possible to achieve creaturely life as God intended it to be. Patience can transform the situation from an occasion for resentment, frustration, or resignation to the disclosure of a whole new range of possibilities and challenges that we might never have glimpsed had not patience afforded leisure for their scrutiny and the determination to persevere until every opportunity had been explored. Patience is a response that is also an inauguration, a new beginning.

Our capacity to be acted upon by others is no less remarkable than our own powers of creativity and action. Our sensitivity and responsiveness, as well as our power to initiate and achieve, surpass those of all other creatures and testify that we are indeed created in the image of God. Many of our best endeavors, not least of all our love for other people, require a human object just as much as a human subject: training an athlete or an artisan, raising a child, undertaking marriage or teaching school or healing the sick.

Furthermore, the person whom we train or marry or teach can contribute equally, as a human model can sometimes bring alive the latent talents of a sculptor or painter. So there is an intimate relationship between the productivity of a community and the responsiveness and patience of those acted upon within it.

In the best of our loving, the responsiveness of the beloved enriches the lover and enables him or her to offer new dimensions of the self, in a spiral of mutual reinforcement that need never have an end. So it is that "they also serve who only stand and waite." These words from John Milton's sonnet "On His Blindness" are spoken by the figure of Patience, who assures those who are "light deny'd" and all others who suffer and are vulnerable that "God doth not need Either man's work or his own gifts, who best Bear his milde yoak, they serve him best." It is a fitting epigraph to Vanstone's own conclusion that we are fellow-sufferers with God, "handed over to the world, to wait upon it, to receive its power of meaning."[10]

The capacity to be affected by others, however, is always double-edged. It can deprive us of ourselves; then there is no mutuality or dialogue but simply the surrender of everything. Perhaps the perils have never been portrayed with greater power than in Arthur Miller's play *Death of a Salesman.* Willy Loman's ambition to be well-liked reflects a culture preoccupied with image at the expense of substance, a world in which a salesman can sell nothing unless he is able to sell himself. For Willy the secret of success can be summarized in seven words: I will be as you desire me. He lives for how he appears in the eyes of others. As age or death or simple indifference closes those eyes one by one, Willy is ever more

diminished because he is in touch with so little else in himself. All that remains is the husk of a man, a smile and a shoeshine and an outstretched hand.

Even if we do not blame Willy Loman but the society that has made him what he is, it is difficult to affirm his dignity as patient, as sufferer. So the dignity of this condition, at least some of the time, is not so much an assurance as a challenge. The world is full of victims who have a claim to dignity because they are all the children of God, but in whose situations as patients there is nothing dignified—unless they make it so. Willy's concern for appearances blinds him to the genuine caring of those around him and incapacitates him so greatly that he is not truly affected by others at all and is incapable of change. In the end, ironically, the ambition to be what he thinks others want him to be leaves Willy shut up within himself with nothing but dreams and illusions, his own prisoner, deprived of the two great goods that true patience requires and reinforces—the capabilities of attentiveness and caring.

Attentiveness and caring are at the center of every form of Christian patience, perhaps even more clearly so than in the case of the other virtues. Their opposites are impatience and indifference or apathy. If we are not attentive and caring to others, we cannot be much affected by them. The two are inseparable and the relationship between them is circular: attentiveness causes us to care and caring causes us to be attentive. The person who is a patient is given the opportunity to pay attention to things, a chance for reflection, contemplation, and self-examination. It is the opportunity to pause, because we rely upon the initiatives of others. Our dependence means we cannot rush further and further without a destination or an end in mind, and we cannot be distracted by incessant busyness and chatter because we must wait for others who may not have arrived. Attentiveness is something we give

to others, but it is also a gift to ourselves that the status of patient affords.

Attentiveness is the foundation of everything else because we can act responsibly and responsively only within the world that we can see. How much we can accomplish depends upon how well we can see: we cannot achieve goals we are unable even to envision or realize possibilities that we have been too impatient to discern. In *The Sovereignty of Good*, Iris Murdoch writes that "the characteristic and proper mark of the active moral agent" is *attention*, a word she borrows from Simone Weil to describe a just and loving concentration upon some individual or situation. We shall never learn to act in measured and judicious ways toward others if we have not learned first of all to pay attention to them. "One is often compelled almost automatically," Murdoch continues,

> by what one can see.... If we consider what the work of attention is like, how continuously it goes on, and how imperceptibly it builds up structures of value around us, we shall not be surprised that at crucial moments of choice most of the business of choosing is already over.... The moral life, on this view, is something that goes on continually, not something that is switched off in between the occurrence of explicit moral choices. What happens in between such choices is indeed what is crucial.[11]

Our initially shapeless freedom comes to be shaped by the presence of other people and, insofar as we can really see them in all their concreteness, our moral decisions are not arbitrary choices but are determined by the sharpness of our vision—our capacity for attentiveness.

It is not easy to see well, however. It is difficult to see objects that move very rapidly or to see in the dark, much less to see interiorities as well as surfaces and penetrate the disguises that

people wear. It is a challenge that bristles with difficulties, Murdoch says, for we are indolent and selfish and unskilled. Writing of complex moral situations in which good answers are far from clear, she comments:

> The love which brings the right answer is an exercise of justice and realism and really looking. The difficulty is to keep the attention fixed upon the real.... Of course virtue is good habit and dutiful action. But the background condition...is a just mode of vision and a good quality of consciousness. It is a task to come to see the world as it is.[12]

Attentiveness means the willingness to pause, to be patient and to become a patient, in order to comprehend a new situation or see an old one afresh.

Therefore, because the capacity for seeing is not easy but a moral skill that must be learned, it needs the time that only patience can provide. Time is the destroyer, but it is also a friend, a healer, the giver of possibilities and renewal, the creator of community and the matrix of new life, and the sphere of God's providential activity. Time means the unfolding of the hidden, the development of the self's powers of discrimination and understanding, precious moments of illumination, room for imagination to roam and leisure for voyages of discovery to unveil what was obscure and to reap the fruits of attentiveness. "Moral change and moral achievement are slow," Murdoch writes, "since we cannot suddenly alter what we can see and ergo what we desire and are compelled by."[13] Patience is the only act of which we are capable that allows the future to disclose what it holds and that prepares us to see what that disclosure means. The waiting that we as patients must embrace can be one of the great human acts of courage and trust. In *Waiting for God* Simone Weil tells us that

> we do not obtain the most precious gifts by going in search of them but by waiting for them. Man cannot discover them by his own powers, and if he sets out to seek for them he will find in their place counterfeits of which he will be unable to discern the falsity.[14]

Attentiveness offers escape from self-absorption and self-deception. It carries us beyond ourselves until the landscape is no longer shadowed by our own preoccupations. It "unselfs" our vision, so to speak. Its adversary is the busyness which can never find time; except for its own chosen commitments, busyness is heedless and finally selfish in its self-affirmation. The world repays our patient attentiveness, revealing what hasty inspection can never fathom. It has countless secrets that are hidden from the casual glance of impatient people whose vision is limited to the surfaces of things. We are unable to care if our only acquaintance with others is fleeting, casual, or manipulative because we are preoccupied with other tasks and with our own welfare. If imagination is tethered to such small and routine concerns, we shall never be able to envision a new and freer existence and so we shall be imprisoned where we are.

Who has a better opportunity than the patient to recognize the interdependence of our lives and, as cared for, to understand the importance of caring? In myself, I am incomplete and limited, dependent, needy, and in some ways powerless. I am created for waiting—for waiting upon others and being waited upon. I must wait for my caring to be reciprocated. I must wait for my turn. I must wait for help. I must wait in the hope that someone will notice me. Therefore where patience leads, humility will soon follow. Attentiveness enables us to care for others as they are and not simply as we would have them be. Caring enables us to be truly attentive to

what is other than ourselves in all its differentness from us. We learn in innumerable ways that we are not the centers of everything. Life is also centered elsewhere. The aims and projects of others for whom we care intrude upon our own, but we must endure these deflections of our purpose and be responsive to others' initiatives and activities if we hope for their responsiveness to ours.

If I know that I am not the center of everything but simply one among many, then I am beginning to learn the difficult lesson that someone else is real, just as real as I. Others are not merely satellites meant to orbit around my greater planet. It is wrong to try to make someone else one's own center, which is the terrible temptation of the lover. The slavish devotion of a mother can enslave her children and consign them to a prison where there is no fresh air to breathe. It is no less wrong to seek to make oneself someone else's center, as husbands often do to their wives or children to parents or aging parents to their offspring. In diverse ways, these imitations of caring are examples of impatience; neither will respect and tolerate the integrity of others. Attentiveness and caring have fallen apart; there is no recognition of difference but only a merging, so caring such as this can breed discontent, rebellion, and even hate. Because the relationship of parent and child is so fundamental, the family is a potential structure of destruction if patience is not present in the house.

When we become patients, dependents, we learn to savor little things that other people so often take for granted: particles dancing in sunlit air, the intricacy of a spider's web, the movement of branches in the wind. Patience gives us the opportunity to appreciate the small ornaments of existence that busyness has neglected. Not least important, it provides an occasion to be alone with oneself but not lonely, because it gives us time to explore within ourselves what is too often unnoticed, hidden, or disguised in the course of our ordinary activities. On the other hand, it is certainly true that illness and pain can sometimes shut us up in ourselves, indifferent to everything and everyone else. Even then, however, the working of grace can sometimes turn us away from our afflictions and beyond ourselves. Dorothee Soelle reminds us of a great truth, which has been emphasized by all the writers we have explored, from Tertullian to Kierkegaard:

> The Christian idea of the acceptance of suffering means something more than and different from what is expressed in the words "put up with, tolerate, bear." With these words the object, the suffering itself, remains unchanged. . . . The word "take," also in its combination with "on, up, over," means that the person doing the accepting is himself changed. What I "take" belongs to me in a different sense from something I only bear. I. . . take on an assignment; I say yes, I consent, I assent, I agree with.[15]

It is often difficult to be a patient and an object, hard to accept our dependence on others, and never easy to receive as gifts what we would much prefer to acquire for ourselves. But perhaps there is no better preparation for hearing the gospel, which is a story about gifts. The recognition of our need to rely on others can cure us of illusions of independence and of the satisfactions of self-reliance and other expressions of pride. Not always and not everywhere, of course, but at some times and in some places the status of patient can bring us the two great goods of sharpened attentiveness and heightened caring, along with the more discerning appreciation and release from selfishness they provide. In such cases the situation has been, at least for the eyes of faith, truly sanctified by God. Then the monologue that busyness encourages is transformed and

existence becomes what it was always intended to be—a conversation.

The theologian Charles Williams captures this vision of our common life when he speaks of our "coinherence" or mutual indwelling. This idea in turn prompts Nathan Scott to speak of the self as one

> whose life requires him to say, "The world is a wedding"—since, everywhere, the horizon encompassing all his plans and projects is one that discloses each mortal soul to be a "peece of the continent, a part of the maine," and this to so profound a degree as to give a kind of heraldic rank to the words of St. Anthony of Egypt, "Your life and your death are with your neighbor."[16]

When attentiveness has finished its painstaking work, the fact of our relatedness has been transmuted into the value of caring about it. We know that mutuality matters.

Thus far, however, we have explored the meaning of patience, and the attentiveness and caring at its core, without examining extensively its relation to other values and disvalues. We have written much about the interdependence and conversation that characterize human life, but treated the virtue that sustains them more or less in isolation, not as part of an interlocking whole. This anomaly must now be corrected, for we cannot grasp the deepest dimensions of the importance of patience without attention to its relationships to the other virtues it supports, as well as to the vices it directly opposes, because of their constant assaults upon attentiveness and caring. Only then will our task be done.

Chapter Seven

Where Patience is Not

impatience, apathy, boredom, displacement

We can know people by the enemies they make and the friends they keep—or so an old adage goes. We shall apply that maxim to patience in this chapter and the next, discussing first its adversaries and then its companions. If the importance of the virtue requires further reinforcement, it can certainly be found in the scores of Christian writers who have chronicled the endless, cruel, and destructive consequences of impatience, beginning with Tertullian's insistence that it is the definitive characteristic of Satan, the temptation to which Eve and Adam first succumbed, and "the cradle" which thereafter becomes "the sole fashioner of all sin," every one of which can be traced back to impatience. If the vice figures so prominently at the origin of our estrangement from God, must not its opposite play a central role in the life of the Christian?

The classical tradition from which the foundations of our notion of virtue are derived has taught the church to understand virtue as a mean between excess and deficiency,

extremes so defective they must ordinarily be seen as vices. Patience stands midway between impatience and apathy, or indifference. The traditional term for the latter vice is insensibility, a word that now has an archaic ring. The authors we have cited are unanimous in their insistence that patience is not always a virtue; it can serve unworthy ends such as greed or revenge. Similarly, neither are all forms of impatience or apparent indifference invariably malicious. There is nothing wrong with the impatience of a prisoner of war eager to escape his confinement and rejoin his comrades in service of a just cause, although there are limits on how such impatience can be expressed. What appears to be apathy may be no more than prudent recognition of territory that lies beyond our powers of intervention in any effective way. We have no right to intrude upon the private affairs of strangers. The messianic determination to save all others despite themselves can become one of the most meddlesome forms of pride, a presumptuous act of interference.

But when impatience fattens and flames into anger because our desires and projects are greeted by indifference or thwarted in some fashion, then it becomes one of the vices traditionally numbered among the seven deadly sins. The ultimate expression of angry impatience is godless defiance of everything that threatens to block an unrestrained and capricious will. The classical tale of Prometheus, who transgressed every limit when he stole the fire of the gods, displays the theological dimension such defiance can assume. In Christian mythology, it is expressed in the rebellious cry of Lucifer, the angelic servant who wanted to be a lord and so became a demon: "I will not serve."

In contrast, true indifference knows neither impatience nor anger nor any other emotion. It does not mean the triumph of reason over passion, the painstaking imposition of discipline

and order upon the unruliness and turbulence of our feelings, but an utterly uncaring spirit. In its most extreme form, indifference is not an attitude we have adopted but a reflection of previous choices, sometimes enforced upon us by circumstances that have numbed and battered us until no capacity for responsiveness remains. For one reason or another, we have habituated ourselves to indifference and become incapable of behaving in any other way. This is why extreme apathy is so terrifying: there can be no appeal from it—it can see nothing and hear nothing. This is the absolute annulment of the dialogue and mutuality and interdependence meant to characterize creaturely life.

The insensible self is someone who is incapable of being affected—lacking all ordinary feelings, unmoved by suffering, and unable ever to shed a tear. The ultimate expression of such indifference or apathy is torpor, *acedie* or sloth, another of the deadly sins. Such indifference is brilliantly portrayed by Albert Camus in his novel *The Stranger,* whose protagonist lives in a world where nothing appears to be significantly connected to anything else. Arrested and tried for a pointless murder that was no more than half intended, and then condemned to die, Meursault's crime in the eyes of his judges seems not to be the killing itself so much as his failure to display any proper grief upon learning of the death of his own mother. But why should he grieve, Meursault wonders; after all, must not everyone die in the end?

It has often been said that the exercise of patience presupposes a more or less just social order. This is a claim that in some sense would have seemed incomprehensible to Tertullian and Cyprian and all the others who extolled the importance of the virtue in times of strife and persecution. But there is a profound relationship between patience and justice, even though the achievement of a just society is certainly not a

prerequisite for the exercise of patience. If that were true, our impatience with injustice would have no chance to learn from patience, and so there would be no restraints upon it. The yoking of the two virtues is important, first of all, because it points to the unity of virtue, which we shall later explore in detail. It is not true that some virtues can be cultivated at the expense of others, as though one could be patient but lack prudence or a sense of fairness. Unless a person possesses all the virtues, she possesses none.

Second, patience is a social virtue, inherently concerned with the neighbor, and so it is essentially different in its Christian form from stoic resignation that triumphs over emotion and looks with suspicion upon all human relationships. Most emphatically, patience is not mere quiescence. It is not indifferent to the claims of social justice and perseveres in its commitment to them, but it knows that no matter how noble the end may be, some means are appropriate and others are not. Thus the ambition to relieve human misery can never justify the temporary increase of the sufferings of the innocent.

Finally, the relationship of the two virtues highlights the opposition between patience and the twin vices—impatience and apathy—that are its extremes. The more just the social order, the greater vice does impatience become, with its insistence upon preferring the self at the expense of other people. The less just the social order, the greater vice does indifference become, because of the way that it inhibits the improvement of the neighbor's condition. Both of them are ultimately centered upon the self.

Impatience sooner or later becomes aggressive invasion of the time and space that belong to others, while apathy is typically the exclusion from consciousness of the claims of others to time and space of their own. The first is covetous, the

second indifferent. They are united in their denial of the essentially dialogical and interdependent nature of human existence. They see no one but strangers. The real problem, however, is not the dismissal of the inescapable fact of our relatedness to one another, but their uncaring rejection of the idea of justice in human affairs. The one is characteristically unjust in its actions; the other does not act because it is deaf to appeals for justice. The first is set on expanding the place of the self and dislocating others from the time and space that were theirs. The second is determined to guard the ostensible borders of the self against all that might open them to calls and claims from other people. This is the reason that both impatience and apathy metastasize into deadly sins: in attacking or ignoring patience, their real enemy is the greatest of the cardinal virtues, the idea of justice.

Neither impatience nor indifference cares for otherness. Habit has blinded them to the claims that accompany the presence of others. Neither knows that someone else is real, just as real as oneself. Impatience is uncaring because its desires fill the whole field of its vision; indifference does not care because its blank gaze transmits so little to the light of consciousness that it affords no access to the chambers of the heart.

My constant refrain has been that patience teaches above all else the mutuality, coinherence, and interdependence of human life. That is the way by which our initially featureless freedom is filled with specific possibilities and challenges. In words so familiar and yet so memorable and poignant still, John Donne reminds us that

> No Man is an Iland, intire of it selfe; every man is a peece of the Continent, a part of the maine; if a Clod bee washed away by the Sea, Europe is the lesse, as well as if a Promontorie were, as well as if a Mannor of thy friends or of

> thine owne were; any mans death diminishes me, because I am involved in Mankinde; And therefore never send to know for whom the bell tolls; It tolls for thee.[1]

The vices speak with one voice; they both insist, "I will not suffer." Impatience regards suffering not as the essential mark of our humanity but as a hindrance to be overcome; apathy has banned it from the precincts of consciousness and therefore surrendered all pretense to moral selfhood. In their different ways, the two shape one world where there is no habitation for anyone except the I, isolated and alone.

The notion that patience is a median between such destructive extremes emphasizes its importance both for the health of the individual and for the development of any sort of community. This idea is valuable because it locates the patient person at a point more or less equidistant between a caricature of the self-sufficiency of God and the formlessness of Proteus, the Greek sea god who could change his shape at will. At one extreme stands the apathetic self—unchanging, self-contained, and self-absorbed, a separate continent washed by no seas whose tides carry messages from other inhabited lands. At the other stands the impatient self whose self-absorption fosters angers and resentments that allow it to be shaped from moment to moment by whatever thwarts the dictates of its imperious will. The impatient self is infinitely variable not by choice but because of an irascibility that deprives it of all the resources to defend itself against external invaders too numerous to count. In the end, impatient self-centeredness leads to the loss of the centeredness of the self. We forfeit what we intend to affirm and imprison ourselves more securely in our vices, utterly vulnerable to everything in the world that stands in our way.

Nevertheless, this interpretation of virtue and vice also has its inadequacies, and two of them are of particular importance.

First, the whole notion that morality can be represented as a mean between extremes suggests there is an element of measuring in the moral life that actually is foreign to it. The good life is not unreflective, certainly, but the reflection it requires is not the calculation of more or less equal distances between evils, but finding the best way to pursue the greatest good. Second, the idea of good as a middle point can tend to obscure the essential motivation for Christian discipleship, which is gratitude for the grace and mercy that God has shown to us in our preservation and reconciliation through Jesus Christ. Christians are called to exercise patience thankfully because God the Father has shown it to them; in all its forms it is the example given to them in the ministry, passion, and death of the Son of God. We are not called to calculation, but to imitation.

The Bible is filled with tales of impatience, which first appears within the gates of paradise itself and then spreads like a contagion to the east of Eden. Like indifference, however, in many ways impatience seems a peculiarly modern sin. One of its causes is simply the crowding of our planet. Once we were pilgrims together; now we are tourists, so to speak, who have little in common and meet in increasingly peripheral and fleeting ways. The difference is that pilgrims engage in a corporate act in the presence of the sacred. Tourists are individuals whose assumptions and values are often in conflict because they are not derived from a shared and sacred whole. Tourists are connected to the world by no firmer bonds than curiosity, and so they impatiently vie with one another for a better view or a place in the sun, a more pleasant site in the park or a quieter table. We are ranged against one another in a thousand small ways. On the one hand, there is community; on the other, the crowd. One is the matrix of moral formation; the other is indifferent to it.

Affluence can enable us to satisfy our impatient desires, to have our turn before others and insulate ourselves from those who have less than we. After all, what is wealth for if it will not buy us the time and space of others that we covet? Contemporary technology so greatly exceeds our capacity to use it productively that impatience flourishes whenever we encounter frustration and delay. Why, we protest, should the master be mastered by the servant? Why value perseverance if the world is a lottery? Why should we prize endurance and the ability to wait if the moment is all, with no horizon beyond the present? Impatiently, we ask what knowledge patience can provide that adds significantly to the information we already have. We tend to forget the difference between knowledge and wisdom, information and the dictates of the heart. Artists, among others, know better: there is no inspiration without perspiration. But it is tempting to forget what common sense teaches.

As we have seen, waiting is as much a part of the human condition as ever it was: waiting for healing to begin, for a child to be born, for casual acquaintance to blossom into friendship or love. The enormous difference is that the waiting once enforced upon us by nature and society and accepted as inevitable now seems unnecessary, an obstacle that resourcefulness and innovation should enable us to overcome, and so we are tempted to become habitually impatient. The end of our century has brought radical changes in our assumptions, to the neglect of patience and luxuriant growth of its opposite—as well as of boredom. Impatience is impatient because it is bored by its location or by the time it must wait. It is too impatient for self-examination or to ask why it is bored and

whether another day or another place or any change at all will offer some remedy for its boredom.

So, if patience is an ancient virtue that has grown unfashionable, perhaps the old vices it opposes have become both more pervasive and more virulent in our time, as well as the condition from which they often emerge and to which they typically lead. Indifference and impatience sometimes travel different roads, but they arrive at the same destination. Its name is boredom. When mere subsistence is a problem, boredom is not; very often it seems a luxury that only the relatively secure and affluent can afford. In a comic passage, Kierkegaard comments on the claim that boredom is the root of all evil:

> The gods were bored, and so they created man. Adam was bored because he was alone, and so Eve was created. Thus boredom entered the world, and increased in proportion to the increase of population. Adam was bored alone; then Adam and Eve were bored together; then Adam and Eve and Cain and Abel were bored *en famille;* then the population of the world increased, and the peoples were bored *en masse.* To divert themselves they conceived the idea of constructing a tower high enough to reach the heavens. This idea is itself as boring as the tower was high, and constitutes a terrible proof of how boredom gained the upper hand. The nations were scattered over the earth, just as people now travel abroad, but they continued to be bored.[2]

How can boredom be overcome? Kierkegaard answers with an analogy drawn from farming: the only antidote is rotation, which has twin forms, extensive and intensive. The first is the search for endless variety, but it ultimately fails because it merely quantifies a problem of quality. Extensive rotation

depends upon constant change. Such is the life of Don Juan, the seducer whose appetite for novelty never encounters anything but repetition and sameness. It is the same self that is imported into each new situation, which becomes as stale and flat as all its predecessors. On the other hand, there is the intensive or true method of rotation for changing crops and the way they are cultivated:

> Here we have at once the principle of limitation, the only saving principle in the world. The more you limit yourself, the more fertile you become in invention. A prisoner in solitary confinement for life becomes very inventive, and a spider may furnish him with much entertainment.[3]

The humor and irony of these comments from *Either/Or* are directed toward the aesthetic life, but their validity is not restricted to the pursuit of pleasure. The busyness of infinite change is a diversion that offers no relief from boredom because it will not acknowledge that the real problem is the transformation of existence. The tools for that are the ability to pause, to stand still rather than always moving on, the willingness to allow others to draw one beyond oneself, leisure for reflection so we can envision what hitherto was not a focus of consciousness and gain a new perspective from which the shape of everything is altered. The only saving principle in the world is limitation: in other words, it is only when our freedom is rendered concrete and specific by the demands of our immediate situation that our freedom becomes significant and creative rather than a prelude to endless repetition and boredom. In responsiveness is our liberation.

Why is boredom the fate of impatient and apathetic selves? Because they can envision nothing beyond themselves. When we have yielded to indifference, we have no obligations except what are imposed from the outside and cannot be evaded.

Because I am a stranger here myself, the vice always insists, every meeting is merely a chance encounter; all of us are simply tourists in a land that no one claims as a permanent residence. We have exiled ourselves from the dialogues and interdependences that could render our liberty important and rewarding, instead of an aimless license to do anything. How could we not grow bored with ourselves when we are no longer willing patients who are transparent and sensitive to other realities? Boredom is entirely shut up within itself. It is no longer a crossroads where diverse realities meet and interact but only a blind alley from which there is no exit. No longer can it afford us fresh and interesting access to anything.

The vices blind us to the fundamental truth that life is conversation—that we are made for conversation—and if we turn our backs to it we are not only impoverishing ourselves but acting against our own inmost nature. So we become far less interesting to ourselves. Because we have banished others from our consciousness, except to acknowledge them as impediments in our path, the whole situation in which we find ourselves has also become less interesting. We have cast ourselves ashore on a desert island where there are no companions except nameless menaces. Self and world are correlative: they are lost together. When an impatient or indifferent self has exhausted beyond replenishment all its own resources, there is nowhere else for it to turn. Despair knows that tomorrow holds merely endless replications of today. So time offers no comfort, and space provides no shelter. The twin structures of creaturely life have become as strange and alien to it as the self has become a stranger and alien to itself.

So it might be said that in losing us, either because of our impatience or indifference toward them, others really lose nothing, while in losing them we have lost ourselves. But the truth is more complex. In depriving others of the room they require for their own development, in rejecting their needs and rights and appeals and attempts at conversation, in trespassing upon the time and space where they have been placed and called to exercise their own distinctive talents, we cause the dislocation of our fellow creatures—and, by so doing, we dislocate ourselves. This is the ultimate work of the two vices that are juxtaposed to patience: they turn both the self and other people into displaced persons.

Displaced persons are the representative figures of our century, with its wretched ethnic conflicts and the scuffling for scarce resources in so many quarters of the globe. Victimized in a thousand ways, displaced persons offer eloquent testimony by their anguished and stricken helplessness that modernity has not domesticated the forces of barbarism. There are far too many groups of them in recent generations to enumerate: Armenians, Jews, Arabs, Hindus, Muslims, Kurds, Khmers, Vietnamese, Rwandans, Croats, Serbs, and many, many more. But displaced persons are not merely the flotsam and jetsam carried by the tides of pestilence, famine, and war in countries far removed from our own. They walk the streets in countless towns and cities, live in our neighborhoods, and sometimes dwell in our own homes. They are not foreigners; they are simply the forgotten and unnoticed.

When a parent is habitually impatient with a child, when children are constantly impatient with aged and infirm parents, when people are dismissive of their colleagues and uncaring of their subordinates, when neighbors are indifferent to the plight of the lonely and handicapped who live on their street—in these and innumerable other ways we create displaced persons in a tranquil and affluent land. In their shared indifference to

patience and the room it always offers other people, the two vices are pervasive sources of the dislocation and dispossession that foster generations of displaced persons. All the more so when they blossom into the deadly sins of anger and sloth. Where once we had neighbors who might have become familiar to us, our actions or inaction have produced a crowd of strangers. The connections among us are contingent, external, and evanescent—sometimes threatening, sometimes inhibiting, but never the source of enrichment.

If modernity has not diminished but intensified the ache and scope of dislocation, certainly one of the prime causes of the increase of indifference is the loss of the neighborhood. It is sometimes as small as a street condemned to suffer the whims of city planners, and sometimes as large as sections of a whole land fractured by ethnic conflicts and urban warfare. The terrible euphemism "ethnic cleansing" designates the expropriation of Catholics and Protestants, Arabs and Jews, Orthodox and Muslims. For reasons great and small we lose a sense of responsibility for those who once lived nearby but whose absence now goes unremarked. We grow inured to mobility, either because we must move from one job to another or because we work for a national or global firm, and so we become less involved with wherever we find ourselves. "Migrant workers" are not simply the harvesters of fruit and vegetables; many of them are senior members of the corporate and academic worlds.

In a commuter culture, the separation between home and workplace drastically limits the time and energy that can be devoted to the welfare of either one. Whether working at home with computers and modems will resolve more problems than it creates is a question that has not yet been determined. So we pass by one another without conversation. We have so many appointments to keep and chores to do and, after all, we are

strangers here ourselves, rootless, temporary, transients in a transient crowd. Busyness is a principal source, reinforcement, and excuse for our indifference; our times are inventive in devising narcotics but we have yet to find any drug more powerful than busyness.

Because the vices treat neighbors as strangers, as those to whom nothing is due, we become foreigners living among foreigners from still other countries whose speech is an unknown tongue. When my brother or sister has become a stranger to me, furthermore, then I have become a stranger to myself. In traditional usage, patience has been equated with self-possession. In other words, we maintain our equanimity and confidence despite all that is visited upon us; nothing is permitted to deprive us of a certain serene composure and the determination to exercise forbearance. The vices that are ranged against patience lead to *dispossession*, the loss of the self. As we lose touch with others we lose touch with ourselves—or, to phrase it differently, because of our isolation there is less and less within us to touch, cherish, and affirm. He who would save his life will lose it. Whoever creates a displaced person is to that same extent dispossessed by the world, and equally displaced.

The eventual plight of the impatient person is well portrayed in *The Sorcerer's Apprentice*, which is a parable about power and technology. The apprentice learns the formula that activates the sorcerer's magic broom but he does not know the words that will still the power he has unleashed. The technology becomes demonic—it assumes a life of its own with an energy that far outstrips the ingenuity of the human imagination to use it for productive ends. The servant brings a certain order where there was modest disorder but then, because the broom is utterly unstoppable, it creates absolute chaos.

In another sense, the story is a cautionary tale about the demonism of impatience and its unavailing flight from

boredom. Just as the vice isolates the self and thereby deprives it of any hope of richness in itself, so does it cause the self to project its own poverty upon the world until there is nothing to prize and savor and conserve. So the self is insatiable for more, impatient to dominate whatever its broom can reach and resentful of whatever eludes its outstretched arm. But nothing it consumes is genuinely satisfying within the throwaway culture it has fashioned; nothing is worth saving, at least not for long. The limitless appetite of impatience is oddly coupled with indifference toward everything it grasps. Since impatience never pauses for reflection or scrutiny, everything grows strange and as shallow as the self itself.

At last we are brought to the condition that Augustine described as *ignorantia et concupiscentia*—ignorance because the self that is made for God searches for infinite Good among an infinitude of finite goods and unbridled hunger because its quest for earthly satisfactions is endless. Bereft of any sort of moral compass, those who are afflicted by the vices in their most extreme forms seek to escape this condition by acting just to see what will happen, for the fun of it, for something to do, to pass the time—which is to say, for no reason at all. This is the mentality of the gangs that aimlessly prowl our urban streets. So it was with Augustine himself, when he stole the pears belonging to his neighbor and threw them to a herd of swine. There was no reason for the act except the pleasure of the lawlessness, the violation, the defiance. In the end, what is left beyond uncaring irresponsibility, absolute indifference, aimless malevolence that has grown impatient even with its own impatience and sense of boredom? Freedom has become featureless and opaque, a burden instead of an opportunity.

What defense has the virtue of patience against all of this? As Calvin and Burroughs, among others, tell us so powerfully, its security and reinforcement lie in the idea of *placement*. From a Christian perspective, a sense of placement is inseparable from faith in providence: the problem is not the absence of God but our reluctance to pause and search for traces of his presence. Placement can be defined as a sense of the human face of providence. All the vices seek to banish providence with their cynical counsel that "God helps those who help themselves." But patience knows that one is not free to help oneself apart from other people. Our freedom is ours because other people have given it to us and helped us shape its proportions, sometimes wittingly and sometimes without knowing what they have done. Freedom is not an endowment. It is a gift. It is, at its richest, a consequence of our placement.

The idea of placement is of fundamental significance for Christian ethics, as few writers have understood better than Martin Luther. Among his greatest contributions to the development of Christian thought was his description of the Christian's calling, or *beruf,* as an inversion of the medieval idea of vocation. In this view all people were summoned to faith in God, and some were called to a special ecclesiastical vocation as priests, monks, nuns, or lay associates of a cloistered order. Luther applied this notion of vocation to the whole range of civil and secular responsibilities that everyone faces, no matter how modest. A priestly calling is different from that of a farmer, soldier, or tradesman, but in no way superior.

One is called to serve God in the here and now, not in some other place or at some other time, and not in some different role or function. Luther's views could be and sometimes were

interpreted in very conservative ways that inhibited social change and individual growth, but only because they were misunderstood. They were of revolutionary importance because of the way they sanctified our common life and related providence to all our affairs. God meets all people equally in, with, and under the secular responsibilities enforced by existence in this place and at this time. The idea of placement acknowledges the hand of God in bringing us to this time and space, and entrusting these other persons—the human face of providence—to dealings with us. So placement is radically different from the notion of "thrownness," a modern term that does not imply obligation or responsibility because it suggests the only rulers of our world are accident and chance. Placement is the foundation for and the result of our most productive and satisfying activity.

We must make our place; it is an achievement as well as a gift. Making our place is an act of freedom, an exercise of responsibility, a willingness to share ourselves with others. Placement is not a possession or an accident of birth. We are placed by others, but we must assent imaginatively and constructively if we are to transform this house into a home. So placement does not mean motionlessness or rest; it is not a static but a dynamic idea because it describes a conversation. It requires constant redefinition and reaffirmation. As children grow and parents age, for example, their needs and relationships also change and must often be appraised anew. So we face the challenge to remake our place, time and again.

Placement has to do with time as much as space, just as the present is a spatial as well as temporal notion. It affirms as strongly as possible the relatedness of the self, whether in our childish dependence or adult mutuality or the frailty of age. Whether we are truly placed in our situation depends upon our responsiveness to whatever the needs of others may be. Our

presence in their world anchors us so that we are no longer adrift. Others give us ourselves. Our freedom is given definition, contours and landmarks, so that it is no longer *terra incognita* but fertile terrain. God's gifts and demands reveal themselves to us only through and in our place, which is intended to be used in ways that will enhance our world and contribute to the increase of community and the achievement of justice.

On the other hand, placement is a gift that is not granted to everyone. We have seen that impatience and indifference create displaced persons. If we have no place of our own our possibilities are radically diminished, because now everything is external to us. We shall remain tourists and wanderers, spiritual vagrants, victims and victimizing transients. There are others, moreover, who are simply in the wrong place. The abuse of children, neglect of the aged, random crime in the streets, sectarian violence, and ethnic cleansing all testify that some people were caught in the wrong place, at least by all human standards. Some can make a place for themselves even in the midst of such suffering, if their presence with and for others contributes to healing and health. But many have every reason to be impatient with their lot and we would be inhumane if we were not also impatient with what they suffer. Impatience is not always a vice. But nothing except patience itself can teach us to know when our impatience is justified, how it can be most productively expressed, and what means are legitimate for it to employ.

Patience is the heart and soul of placement, the foundation for everything else, because it is fundamental to our interacting with others and suffering their initiatives. It means that our own poverty is enriched by all the other people who are offered some sort of habitation in our own minds and hearts. These strangers become familiars and partners in our internal conversations, instructing and challenging and admonishing and comforting long after they have forgotten us or died or found a new address. The great work of patience is the transformation of strangers into neighbors by accepting their initiatives and responding with our own, so that we are enriched by their indwelling in us and able to offer our own contributions to the community through our indwelling in them.

Long before it is a virtue, patience is simply an acknowledgment of the way things are. There is nothing we can do to alter our condition. No feat of genetic engineering will change decisively the dependence and mutuality that characterize our humanity. Mutuality means that everyone is at least potentially a neighbor. We dwell together in a world intended to grow ever more familiar because together we have been appointed by God its stewards and overseers. The operative word is "together," for God's gracious offer of dominion is depends upon our willingness not to exercise domination and so displace others. Our potential creativity—our power *to*—is achieved only by way of drastic limitations upon our power *over*, which subverts the reciprocity, supportiveness, and mutuality upon which our fulfillment depends.

The first place we find ourselves is within the family. Of all the forms of patience such intimacy requires, forbearance is the most important. Where it is absent, children must look elsewhere for the support they must have as they face the challenges the world presents. Apart from forbearance and its capacity for reconciliation, placement means nothing but imprisonment. Such patience imitates the works of God, who does not begrudge us the time and space we need to exercise our strengths and express our creativity—and who then comes to restore the gifts that we have wasted and misused. Such acts of reconciliation are the highest form of creativity we know,

because they produce transformed lives rather than mere artifacts or insubstantial ideas. The greatest creativity, both divine and human, has to do with persons, not with things. So we are told, "When you are offering your gift at the altar, if you remember that your brother or sister has something against you, leave your gift there before the altar and go; first be reconciled to your brother or sister, and then come and offer your gift" (Matthew 5:23-24).

Reconciliation means the reunion of the separated, the reestablishment of familiarity and support where those who once were close have become strangers and displaced persons. The restored relationship is richer and stronger than the original, for it is a victory over misunderstanding or one sort of betrayal or another. It is liberating, for it frees us from the prison of the past and lets us begin afresh, wiser than we were before. Patience has an absolutely fundamental role in all of this, for without the endurance and forbearance it signifies love could never attain this supreme expression. There can be no reconciliation, and therefore no liberation, and so no truly creative act, where patience has not provided room and found a place.

Despite St. Paul's assertion in the first letter to the Corinthians that Christian love is always patient, much of our loving is more intent upon saving vulnerable people from peril than on providing them room to breathe. In *Crime and Punishment* Dostoyevski tells the story of the Grand Inquisitor, a cardinal of the church whose love for those entrusted to his care leads him to offer them bread instead of freedom. Bread always nourishes but freedom is never without the potential for disappointment and harm. The cardinal is undone by his own compassion, persuaded that it is better to offer certainties to those he loves rather than confessing doubts that would confuse and demoralize them. It is better to bind them to him

than to leave them on their own in a darkening world. Perhaps the most difficult lesson any man or woman must learn is to let a spouse or child or other loved one have room; the greater the love the more difficult it is either to offer or to accept this gift of freedom. Love can stifle and suffocate both lover and beloved if it is not shaped and ordered by constant patience.

So St. Paul insists that the very first work of love is patience. Christian love is inseparable from justice, and patience is the bridge by which they are joined. Such love reflects the benevolence of a Creator who never crowds or hurries the creatures he has made. Love and justice fall out with one another when patience is not vigilant in the defense of what justice requires. To insist that patience is love's first work, then, is to affirm that love and justice are two sides of the same coin.

Why is it written in 1 Corinthians 13 that love is not only patient but kind? What new element does kindness contribute? Part of the answer is that patience can be exercised, as we know, in sterile as well as fruitful ways. It is not invariably a good even when formed by love, because some loves are no more than selfish attempts to assure the continuation of our lives through others. The patience we show others in order that they might become more like us is no virtue but a work of pride, and as great a vice as impatience. Nor can patience without justice display the kindness that is committed to diversity, to difference, to novelty and genuine change. Human patience is meant to reflect in some small way the forbearance of the God who made men and women to offer their own distinctive contributions, not only in what they produce but in who they are. Patient love is kind because it guards the time and space of others so that they may become whatever they choose to become, in their own way and at their own pace. Patient love is kind because it hopes for genuine diversity and novelty, not mere replication. It does not ask that sons become in all ways like their

fathers, or daughters copies of their mothers. It does not say one must live where one was born, or travel the same paths an earlier generation did.

This chapter has incorporated many themes. We began with impatience and indifference as great and deadly sins when they grow into anger, resentment, or sloth. Impatience and indifference make us vulnerable to boredom and eventually to despair and the loss of the self, conditions that are reinforced by developments in the contemporary world. The ultimate outcome of these vices is the creation of displaced persons, those paradigmatic figures of the twentieth century, and our own impoverishment because we deny the dependence written into the deepest part of our nature.

It has often been remarked that God is in the details, and this Christian people should affirm. But the devil is in the details, too, or else we would never need to worry about the congruence of means and ends. Is it possible to see a direct relationship between the impatience and indifference we see all around us every day in the details of our ordinary activities, and the brutalities humankind has inflicted upon itself in the course of this century? Can such great and horrific events emerge from such small beginnings, such minor and mundane details? Can the mutation from microcosm to macrocosm be so simple, so linear and direct? That has been the implicit argument in this chapter. Habituation to the most trivial forms of the vices can begin a process of moral hardening that will eventually lead us into complicity with terrors that were at first beyond imagining. Such is the banality of evil: from the smallest of beginnings arise consequences that are wholly unforeseen, unintended, and irreparable. Wherever patience is absent, nothing might happen, or anything could occur.

Chapter Eight

The Unity of Virtue

humility, gratitude, and thanksgiving

In the Rijksmuseum in Amsterdam hang many of Rembrandt's most famous paintings, including *The Anatomy Lesson of Dr. Joan Deymon,* in which the physician soberly instructs those less experienced than he in the orderly messiness of the human body. The doctors of virtue have done much the same for two and a half millennia, following the ambition of Plato to carve reality at the joints, cutting through muscle and membrane to expose the structure of its frame. Some of the allure of the theory of virtue lies in its apparent simplicity—the distinctions between theological and natural virtues, between greater and lesser, between life governed by reason and life at the mercy of unruly passions. But these distinctions fail to carve reality at the joints. Virtue is a living body, and anatomy lessons can be practiced only when life is gone.

Let us explore four claims about patience that illustrate the ways in which the actual untidiness of the life of virtue eludes the anatomist's skills. Each reveals further the importance of

patience in relations with both neighbor and God. First, *patience is an essential ingredient of every virtue.* That is why the assaults that impatience and indifference launch against it are actually attacks upon all the virtues without exception. For that reason these vices are deadly indeed. Even the most ordinary experience tells us that without patience, there is no virtue. Writers such as Gregory I referred to patience as the root and guardian of all the virtues; Lactantius and Tertullian as well as others asserted it was the chief or highest among them. Because patience is an essential part of every virtue, it is a *sine qua non* for all community, both human or divine, an achievement of the self and equally a gift beyond human attainment.

Patience is not only the handmaiden of *justice* but an essential element within it. Others must be given room for the expression of their freedom. This means that their initiatives will impinge upon our liberty; for better and for worse, we must endure their activities with equanimity. They must also be given the time to develop in accordance with their own interests, strengths, and personal calendars. We must be forbearing of the wastefulness and missteps this can involve; if we impatiently try to set their pace for them, we are not attentive to or respectful of their difference from us. True justice toward others involves the patient expectancy that challenges them to be and to do more than they would ever achieve otherwise. Our patience toward others is enabling for them, just as the forbearance of God and family and peers has been enabling for us. If we have no patience, we will have robbed them of their proper time and space, the necessities that justice toward them is intended to protect.

Similarly, *courage* has no meaning if it does not entail the patience to endure adversities calmly. But there is also a more active side of patience that courage demands, expressed in the perseverance that will not abandon the task at hand or betray

the sense of perfection of a performing artist. Courage includes the patient determination to see a project through to the end, refusing to forsake it, no matter how great the odds, while there still remains a chance that expectant waiting will be rewarded. The idea of *prudence* without patience is foolish, for it would mean that prudence had imprudently discarded one of its essential resources. Prudence determines what virtue requires at a particular time and place, and when there might be new opportunities for the amelioration of things. As the willingness to wait without the loss of hope, patience enables prudence to determine when the time is right, or else to endure calmly and practice forbearance until the dawn of a better day. It provides the time that vision demands; its attentiveness and willingness to pause allow prudence to comprehend all the dimensions of its situation and find undiscovered possibilities there. As persistence or perseverance, patience can work to transform the situation into one more amenable to the pursuit of justice. Then prudence can accomplish more than it first envisioned.

Temperance also demands patience. We will never mature and grow without the patience to discipline the immaturity that tolerates no restrictions upon its desires and has not yet learned that it must forego immediate gratification and wait for its proper turn. We must practice attentiveness to the whole range of powers and potentialities within us, even to those we do not immediately recognize, because without such patience and the pauses it provides, there is no hope for the wholeness that temperance seeks. Patience means learning to say no to passions, impulses, and inclinations that seek too quickly to dominate one another, sorting them out so that most of our resources can be marshaled in the service of whatever is worth persistent and focused effort. It counsels us to wait because we are not ready, or are too impulsive, or have chosen the wrong time, or have failed to see that other things must come first.

We must also be patient with ourselves, as Thomas à Kempis so wisely counsels; we must show forbearance toward ourselves—though this is surely not to excuse all our behavior, our rationalizations and self-deceptions. If only for the sake of the God who created us, we must not be too harsh with ourselves, for perhaps our skills and intelligence and strength are simply not equal to the goals we have set for ourselves. If we are not patient with ourselves, then the sphere of our activities will become ever more limited to what is easily achievable, the weight of the past and its failures will grow ever more difficult to bear, and fulfillment will be unattainable. The way from unruly childishness to temperate maturity is never traveled without the companionship of patience.

Wherever patience is absent, *love* sours, leaving no more than a dreadful parody of itself. For the sake of love we endure as much as we must, as calmly and patiently as we can. We are forbearing and forgiving toward those we love and who love us; no matter how often our expectations are disappointed, we do not surrender our hope that patience will be rewarded. Love also involves constancy and consistency. Those we love must have the confidence that they can depend on us, especially the children who will not otherwise gain the basic trust that is essential for their development. If we grow impatient, we will no longer love and cherish the otherness of others, their remarkable difference and separateness from ourselves. Love and the attentiveness of patience go hand in hand, for love always seeks to discover more of the depths and richness of the beloved. It is in the love for God which grace engenders that one sees most clearly the coinherence of patience and love: the willingness to endure the loss of everything the human heart holds dear for the sake of the love of God. Love is a commitment to patience, everywhere and always.

What could be the meaning of *hope* if it were not patient? Its heart and soul is the readiness to endure the present in the expectation that tomorrow will offer more than today. Hope is greatly diminished if we are unwilling to persist and persevere, for then there would be no reason to hope for the fruits of self-reliance, the outcome of our own industry and discipline. How could we hope for the help of others if we were not forbearing and patiently supportive, offering them their proper turn so that we can also expect our own? Or how could hope anchor itself firmly in reality if it were not prepared to search its situation for the new values and possibilities that only attentiveness and empathetic regard can discern? Patience sees what indifference and boredom never can, because it takes the time, dedicates the energy, and wants to see. Patience and despair may look upon identical landscapes and at first glimpse nothing that promises renewal or relief. Yet patience lives between memory and anticipation in such a way that it brings something to the situation that was not apparent until patience has done its careful work. So there are still grounds for hope as long as life shall last. Patience, even when its own vision is obscured, can try to clothe itself with the imaginations of others and thus hope to find new images of hope.

Finally, *faith* would be faithless were it not for patience, without which it would not endure. Faithfulness to our Creator constrains us to display to others the same patience God has shown to us in our creation and reconciliation. How could we offer to our fellow creatures less than what we ourselves have received: ungrudging patience continually renewed? Faith in the Creator demands unwearying and persevering effort in the confidence that the universe we have been given is a benign and appropriate context for the exercise of human liberty. Faith in Father and Son together emboldens us to endure patiently the adversity we encounter, in imitation of the Suffering

Servant who was obedient unto death. As a synonym for Christ's obedience, patience is the content of faith. In the time between the times we must be ready to pause, to listen in confident expectancy, so that we can attentively discern and decipher the signs of God's activities in our lives.

Anatomy lessons, therefore, tell us far less than we need to know about the living body of virtue. There are no virtues without patience. Each requires every attribute of patience—calm endurance, expectant waiting, forbearance, and perseverance— and, in their Christian versions, a pervasive note of gratitude. Patience is many things: a necessity that our nature enforces, a requirement of civic order, an ingredient of every virtue. It is one of the most selfless and significant acts of which the human spirit is capable, and the heart of the gospel. Without it, the world has

> ...really neither joy, nor love, nor light,
> Nor certitude, nor peace, nor help for pain;
> And we are here as on a darkling plain
> Swept with confused alarms of struggle and flight
> Where ignorant armies clash by night.[1]

The second claim about patience is simply the obverse of the first. If patience is an ingredient in each of the principal virtues, both natural and theological, then *all the virtues reside in patience itself*. Patience would not be genuine if it did not include each and every one. This inclusiveness is the difference between the true article and its counterfeits; it is what distinguishes true patience from all the twisted and truncated forms that abound in our world. Attentiveness may enable patience to see more broadly and deeply than indifference or haste or rashness, but it cannot teach patience to see everything, or even all that it must if it is to be true to itself. It must look to the other virtues of which it is a part and which are parts of it in order to understand its own role. There is no true patience where one or more of the other virtues is absent from it; it requires all of them for its own health.

If patience does not know what justice teaches, for example, it can condone the poor's lack of opportunity, isolate itself from the appeals of the defenseless, and become an accomplice of the unbridled exercise of power. Then patience is no better than indifference. Similarly, if it does not comprehend what courage involves, it can find excuses to shrink from the risk that self-development entails, never persevering in exploring the whole spectrum of our potential or committing itself to values that transcend self-interest. If patience does not understand the meaning of temperance, it will be endlessly tempted and distracted and deprived of its self-possession. Without prudence, it will not know when patience is warranted and when it is not; it will not be able to tell whether perseverance in a certain task is appropriate or beyond our strength. Without all that hope affords, patience will have no real justification for its endurance and willingness to wait, and it will have lost its reasons for forbearance and perseverance. No longer able to discern the workings of providence, patience will be no more than acquiescence, mute resignation. Without faith, it loses all its strongest incentives. Memories of treachery and betrayal will sap its willingness to forbear and forgive. Finally, without love, it will attempt nothing beyond its own defense and security in the midst of a hostile universe.

Again we encounter the truth that virtue is a living unity, an organism of many parts from which nothing can be removed without the loss of the whole. Every anatomy lesson furnishes an artificial picture of what is alive only when it is part of the

whole. As an integral part of all the virtues, patience must be interpreted in the light of the whole that it supports and that participates in it. It is neither autonomous nor does it serve different masters, as though a distinct patience were demanded by separate virtues with their own independent fiefdoms, so that it would not need to busy itself with a larger context. In the end, virtue is a seamless garment like its master's robe. That is why its cultivation requires, apart from the other operations of grace, such enormous patience.

This second claim—that all virtues come together in patience—is the foundation of a third. At first glance, this claim seems quite odd: *patience can be a vice as well as a virtue, and impatience can be a virtue as well as a vice.* These reversals offer their own testimony to the importance of patience, which can give birth to its apparent opposite in order to serve the will of God. Thus patience can say that the time for patience is gone. Sometimes we must be impatient, and express our impatience with clarity, courage, and passion in the face of injustice and brutality. Paradoxically, nothing except patience itself can enable us to *pause,* take our time, so that we can discern the times and places where impatience is appropriate and how it can best be expressed. Patience is the adoptive parent of justifiable impatience; patience both sanctions and restrains our impatience. When impatience comes unstuck from patience it is heedless and rash. Patience teaches it to count the cost, lest it compound the evils of tyranny or repression. Patience insists that even the most noble and urgent ends will not justify every means.

And yet we must be vigilant lest our patience become indistinguishable from indifference to things we should firmly

oppose. Everything in our fallen world is susceptible to corruption and misuse. All our highest values and sincerest pieties can be held in unrighteousness, and patience not least of all. Tertullian and Augustine and countless others warn that it can be employed in the service of vicious ends: we can exhibit extraordinary patience in our determination to destroy a career or ruin a reputation. We can devote all our patience to the promotion of our own prospects without a moment's sympathy for those who must be swept from our path. Few things marshal the resources of patience more than the intensity of our desire for revenge. Patience can be an awesome and terrible adversary when it is enlisted in the cause of jealousy or envy or hatred or random cruelty. Patience can indeed move mountains. Therefore, we must never underestimate its power in the hands of those who crave, in one set of circumstances or another, a final solution.

Patience can also be an expression of pride when we are determined to create others in our own image, to raise children who are mirrors of ourselves, to freeze future generations in our own moral and political stance. Pride is part of our impulse to patronize others: we will be patient because they are not as intelligent as we, or as sensitive, or as successful, and we will be patient in ways that leave them in no doubt of how inferior we believe them to be. So patience becomes not enabling but inhibiting, a tool of domination. Then, too, there is patience as weakness: the harried admonition to be patient is simply a desperate appeal to be left alone, shut up within our preoccupations.

One can argue quite correctly that all these are twisted and defective forms of patience, not really patience at all, because they have clearly lost any relation to justice. But the real problem lies much deeper. Ideological taint means that within society patience always faces the peril that it will fall into apathy

or callousness. Appeals to show patience are so often nothing but demands to surrender moral selfhood, accept the tyrannies of the day, and wink at the injustice and oppression that others suffer. The posture of considered patience can deafen us to the entreaties of our neighbors, convincing us that this is not our battle, that this is a challenge for others, that we should not be involved, that we have more urgent business.

We know that for evil to triumph all that is necessary is for good people to do nothing. But might not the dangers be averted if we are sufficiently patient? What would be the difference, in any event, if we were to join the struggle—for how much can one individual achieve? So we deceive ourselves into thinking that patience is preferable to involvements that are futile and doomed. We may not deceive others, but we can certainly deceive ourselves; the blindness and ignorance and insensitivity that patience fosters are no less real because they are self-engendered. In the end, we are content to be bystanders, indifferent to injustice, unable to see reasons why we should be other than we are. In such ways can patience entail self-deceptions and a blindness to our neighbors and the dignity of their struggles.

We cannot deny the fact that patience expresses a certain bias toward the way things are. It is inherently conservative. It may confidently expect a new world, but it does not hurry out to dismantle the present one. Why should it counsel endurance with serenity and good cheer if, in fact, the situation is insupportable? Why value perseverance unless what has already begun is worthwhile? What reasons are there to exercise forbearance if the present is so wretched that its architects seem unforgivable? Why should we pause and scrutinize the contemporary shape of things if it is all a wasteland where no flower will ever bloom? Patience never despairs of the present; it never wants to raze all the edifices earlier generations erected in order to build the New Jerusalem. It believes the present is a work of providence and placement in it reflects God's own design. The discrediting of the idea of patience in the nineteenth century was in significant part the consequence of a perceived ideological taint: a widespread quietism that would not challenge oppressors in their victimization of those weaker than they. But this involves a great misunderstanding.

Not only can patience sanction impatience, it is the only legitimization that impatience can possess. That legitimization does not qualify or relativize the cruciality of patience itself, but most powerfully reinforces it. Impatience can be a true act of discipleship, not faithless contempt for the way things are nor a rash refusal to wait until the time is right. There is a very great place for impatience in the modern world. There are so many outrages that cry out for instant remedy or at least amelioration. Perhaps we might endure them ourselves, but it is unendurable to see them visited upon others whose condition we have the power to improve. Confronted by genocide, starvation, slavery, the abuse of children, gross corruption in high places, the shameless displacement of whole peoples, random violence, and casual brutality, all of us are sometimes called to be most passionately and profoundly impatient for Christ's sake. When the self is involved with others in such situations and not suffering alone, patience is no virtue and the Christian tradition can say not a single word in its defense. It is well to remember that the New Testament writers scarcely portray Jesus himself as a paragon of patience in their story of his time in the temple that he described as a den of thieves, when he overturned the tables of the money changers and drove from its precincts the sellers of sacrificial birds and animals.

On the other hand, we must never simply put patience behind us, because we will not know what to do without the

lessons it teaches. Only the person who has been schooled in patience and learned its lessons well is capable of instructed impatience. Because patience bears all the greater virtues within itself, the patient individual will act in just and courageous and prudent ways. How could we know when impatience is really justified if patience did not tell us so? How could we know what expressions of impatience are truly just and faithful and prudent unless patience is our guide, reminding us that worthy ends can never justify a whole range of unworthy means? What is godly impatience and what is mere self-indulgent, self-righteous posturing? Patience understands the magnitude of the distinction. Impatience as a vice is always proud, unjust, and egocentric, uncaring of others. Impatience as a virtue is always selfless, prudent, and expressed in defense of justice. The chronically impatient person does not have a clue about when there is no alternative to impatience without the loss of moral selfhood, or about how such impatience can be most productively exercised. Impatience has no moral authority except when it is the principled expression of a person learned in patience.

There is a long way to travel between recognizing what merits our impatience—which is frequently not at all difficult to do—and understanding what attitudes and actions are legitimate expressions of a sense of outrage and are thus warranted in some specific situation. In the course of such travel there are many perils. For example, Kierkegaard has written of suddenness as an epiphany of the demonic—by which he means something wholly inappropriate, incommensurate with what the situation might warrant, never suggested by a person's prior conduct. It is demonic because it is not so much an expression of flawed character as a stepping completely out of character, something unprecedented and without context, a flash of lightning across a cloudless sky. No matter how greatly justified impatience may be, no matter that nothing else would be even imaginable for a moral person, there are always demons at hand ready to transform principled impatience into heedlessness and impetuosity, seductively whispering that the end will surely justify the means.

Patience educates us so we can be vigilant in our impatience, lest it sour or spoil or cloak the quiet atheism that assumes there are no actors on the stage except ourselves, no intimations of the workings of God, and nothing impermissible in the face of such great evil. At least from a Christian perspective, patience frequently has a crucial role to play as the support and companion of virtuous impatience, and therefore it must never be viewed as though it were necessarily conservative, much less reactionary, any more than impatience is invariably progressive and potentially revolutionary. Consequently, it is wrong to suspect patience of an inherently ideological bias when it ventures into social and political affairs, for it can lead to impatience for Christ's sake as well as bring forth its own proper fruits. In its relationship to impatience, the virtue of patience discloses still another dimension of its importance and enduring commitment to fair play.

The fourth claim about patience is that, just as patience introduces us to a world in which the self is never left to itself, so also does patience never travel without company. In Christian perspective, *patience is inseparable from humility and gratitude.* These three, like faith, hope, and love, are also in some sense one. If patience directs us toward the larger virtues in order to understand what patience itself means, so it orients us also toward the smaller companions, such as humility, which Thomas Aquinas canonized as the most important theological

virtue after faith, hope, and love. Although there has been no firm and enduring consensus about the number or relative significance of the lesser virtues, humility and gratitude require special attention because of their inseparable relationship with patience. *The Oxford English Dictionary* defines humility as "having a lowly opinion of oneself; meekness, lowliness, humbleness; the opposite of pride or haughtiness." It cites a seventeenth-century author who captured the sense of tradition when he commented in 1639 that true humility is to have "a meane esteeme of himselfe out of a true apprehension of Gods greatnesse." The reference to God is absent, however, in the dictionary's citation of words that David Hume wrote a century later: "Humility... is a dissatisfaction with ourselves on account of some defect or infirmity." This secularization of the virtue is also evident in the companion definition of the word humble as "having a low estimate of one's importance, worthiness, or merits; marked by the absence of self-assertion or self-exaltation; lowly: the opposite of proud."[2]

Humility is not numbered among the constituents of the classical Greek ideal of *arete*, the intrinsic fineness of the spirit, but is a distinctively Christian and stubbornly theological idea that bristles with problems when it is transplanted to a secular context. It is an effect of grace that presupposes God's self-disclosure because the sole and exclusive measure of our "meane" condition is "a true apprehension of Gods greatnesse." In its conventional form humility seems the least fashionable of virtues, for ours is the era of advertising, and self-advertising is among the age's most powerful and pervasive styles. What is deemed important is perception and not reality. Little seems more socially dysfunctional than everyday humility. In Christian perspective, however, because it is a stubbornly theological virtue its focus is first of all upon God and on the self in relation to God. It is not a secular comparative judgment upon the worth of the self in relation to other people, an acknowledgment of the modesty of the self's own accomplishments and talents in comparison with those of someone else. When it is understood in such worldly terms, the pursuit of humility will not free the self from egocentricity but will actually reinforce it.

In *The Screwtape Letters,* C. S. Lewis shrewdly comments on the way that conventional notions of humility become strategies of the devil. If the virtue is misinterpreted as though it were a secular comparison, we will have placed the self once again in the center of the picture and put true humility to flight. Our fallen condition will grow all the more onerous because the quest for selflessness will have betrayed us into even greater preoccupation with ourselves. In a series of letters a senior devil named Screwtape reviews satanic wiles with his apprentice Wormwood and contrasts them with the aims of God, "the Enemy":

> By this method thousands of humans have been brought to think that humility means pretty women trying to believe they are ugly and clever men trying to believe they are fools. And since what they are trying to believe may, in some cases, be manifest nonsense, they cannot succeed in believing it, and we have the chance of keeping their minds endlessly revolving on themselves in an effort to achieve the impossible.[3]

If the lowly opinion of ourselves that humility denotes is not a mere sense of inadequacy or habitual sadness or distaste for ourselves, still less is it a dismissive and ungrateful denial of the richness of human nature and our possibilities as creatures made in the image of God.

Humility ascribes all of the self's worth and the worth of its projects to God. It is the opposite of willfulness, of ambitions to

self-determination, and the non-dialogical existence that is turned inward upon the isolated individual, because humility prefers others to itself. The *Oxford English Dictionary* definition of the virtue is greatly flawed because it focuses upon the solitary individual without also including a meaning far more familiar within the Christian tradition: preferring others to oneself. This has the merit of stressing that humility is not only a social virtue but among the most important of them. As a theological virtue, then, humility determines the nature of social relations but it does not involve any secular comparisons. Preferring others to oneself can be the most powerful of incentives to accomplish great tasks and hold positions of high authority on the part of humble people who understand power not as domination but as the opportunity for service.

Humility transforms self-love; it does not curb or relativize love for the self, much less uproot it. Bernard of Clairvaux writes of a stage of Christian spirituality in which we no longer love the self for itself but only for the sake of God. The obverse of the matter is that one *must* love the self for the sake of God, for it is created and sustained and affirmed by him. Because humility sees the self in relation to God, it furnishes the strongest imaginable warrant for self-love, a foundation that nothing at all could ever destroy, not even the absolute worst that we can do to ourselves. There is still reason to regard ourselves with wonder as God's own creatures, and to praise the Creator of something so finely and remarkably wrought.

Screwtape counsels Wormwood to consider "the Enemy's strategy." God wills the transformation of egocentric love of the self into appreciation of it as the culmination of the whole process of creation:

> The Enemy wants him, in the end, to be so free from any bias in his own favor that he can rejoice in his own talents as

> frankly and gratefully as in his neighbor's talents. . . . He wants each man, in the long run, to be able to recognize all creatures (even himself) as glorious and excellent things. He wants to kill their animal self-love as soon as possible; but it is His long-term policy, I fear, to restore to them a new kind of self-love—a charity and gratitude for all selves, including their own; when they have really learned to love their neighbors as themselves, they will be allowed to love themselves as their neighbors.[4]

Humility is filled with wonder as it reflects on the beauty and utter self-sufficiency of God and the unfathomable mystery that, although rich and complete in himself, God yet determines to create humanity, give it a realm for the free expression of all its potential, and deputize it to exercise stewardship over this whole creation. The wondering humility engendered by all this is empowering, a reason for creativeness and not sterile restraint, for inventiveness is part of our appropriate gratitude that we might be at play in the fields of the Lord. How is it that those who are so lowly in comparison to God should be accounted worthy of such a gift? The only proper response is humility and gratitude. How is it that our stewardship is allowed to continue, after we have remorselessly spoiled it in so many ways? The only proper response is thanksgiving, humility, and contrition. Gratitude and contrition are no less inseparably united with humility than is patience.

Contrition is always the companion of humility because the fundamental contrast we encounter is not between creature and Creator, but between the holiness and righteousness of God and the unrighteousness and arrogance of the sinner. The disproportion is not so much metaphysical as it is moral, for God is the giver of the law. Humility is a specifically Christian virtue

not simply because it was awarded no lodging within the household of Aristotelian ethics, but in the far more important sense that it constrains the self to see itself always in relation to the law of God. Patience knows that freedom is sterile and without significance until it is landscaped and contoured by the presence of others. Humility acknowledges the further determination and concreteness that freedom gains from the Decalogue and the counsels and precepts of the gospel.

Humility recognizes the folly of the ambition to be like gods, ripping away the center of our existence from God and seeking instead to place the self there. So humility can be the guardian and sustainer of patience: it is the curb upon our impulses to rashness, suddenness, recklessness, haste, heedlessness, and impetuosity, all of which are expressions of irritated vanity. It is the ultimate remedy for the impatience that Tertullian believed was our original sin. If forbearance toward ourselves and others does not express what humility has acknowledged through acquaintance with the law of God, then it is no better than the permissiveness that is quite incapable of teaching any of the lessons moral development requires, contrition being first among them. Nor is perseverance a virtue if it is unaccompanied by the humility that acknowledges limitations.

Preferring others to the self has nothing to do with the absence of the healthy self-love that, divested of the selfishness and anxiety about tomorrow that betoken estrangement, is appropriate for one who is cherished and affirmed by God the Creator. As Lewis reminds us, it has even less to do with absurd mental contortions intended to persuade us that anything we can do others can do better. On the contrary, humility teaches us to love ourselves not only better but *more*, strange as that may seem, precisely because it will look nowhere except to God and ourselves in relation to God, not to the thoughtless and tawdry ways in which we betray ourselves. It is empowering

because it will never allow us to become lost in the shabbiness of our past. What preferring others means is safeguarding and furthering the diversity that is the Creator's design, else he would not have called into being creatures as different from himself as we. It is a determination to allow and enable others to be truly other than ourselves, refraining from playing god for them. It is not at all merely a matter of who will accumulate a few more of the world's goods or an extra scrap of ephemeral recognition. But it is far from the tolerance that actually believes in nothing, for it has gone to school before the mirror of the law of God and so it recognizes the moral limits upon the ambition to foster and sustain difference and diversity.

Patience uses the leisure it discovers in order to hone its attentiveness so that it can see more broadly and deeply than impatience can. Humility is busy clearing away obstacles that can distract and diminish the powers of sight that patience wants to employ, and the principal obstacle is the self. No other virtue is so transparently an effect of grace. We can struggle to increase our patience and succeed admirably, but when humility is our goal the endeavor will eventually defeat its own ambition. True humility seems to catch us unaware; not only does it come from outside but we are quite unconscious of what we have received. Now the I no longer has the I obstructing its vision, its shadow obscuring the proportions of whatever it is attempting to regard. No longer are we distracted and blinded by the ubiquity of a self that appears hopelessly and inextricably entangled with everything else because its egocentricity and desires prevent it from seeing anything independent of the self.

Humility is our great exorcist and iconoclast, sweeping the secular realm free of its religious demons, for it acknowledges not only some worldly distinctions but the infinite qualitative difference between the whole creation and its Lord. The Latin root of humility is *humus,* which means of the earth, earthly,

ground. It is related to the word for man, *homo.* Humility knows that humans and all their values and projects and accomplishments are never more than of the earth, earthly, and will someday return to the dust from which they came. Therefore, it recognizes that this world is not full of gods, that there is nothing truly sacred within the secular, and that we must always restrain ourselves from ungodly temptations to dominate others in the name of some false absolute. Humility knows that it has nothing of which to boast except in the cross of Christ, and much for which to be contrite when it sees its low estate in the mirror of God's law.

Humility has no objection to being considered almost last of all. Because its whole orientation is toward God, it provides no room for self-assertion or undue self-seriousness. Patience's knowledge that life is suffering and that there is little we have not received from others gains new resonance from humility's ascription of everything to God's gracious work. Although the notion of *arete* and the anatomy of the principal virtues is plunder taken from the Gentiles, the inclusion of humility in the list of virtues endows them with a Christian stamp of which the architects of *arete* never dreamed. Now the quest for human excellence is accompanied by the disclosure of divine law and can be fulfilled only by way of preferring others to the self. If patience sees the affinities between the disciple and the sage, humility—which Aristotle could never understand except as a vice—tells us how different they will always remain.[5]

As suffering the initiatives of others which enable me to grow and exercise my freedom, patience certainly has reason for gratitude, and gratitude for all these gifts from others inspires still greater patience toward them. As acknowledgment of our lowliness before the Creator who affirms and cherishes and sustains us nonetheless, humility is the source of gratitude, and thankfulness for so much that is undeserved reinforces humility. At its most comprehensive, gratitude is an attitude toward the giver, a sense of obligation, and an attitude toward the gift, a determination to use it well, to employ it imaginatively and inventively in accordance with the giver's intention. Gifts are reasons for rejoicing. They are also motives for action. Therefore, gratitude becomes a virtue akin to justice; it is resolved to respond freely and appropriately to the giver in ways that display elements of humility and patience.

Patience and humility and gratitude form a triad of virtues analogous to faith and hope and love; after these, they are the most important of the theological virtues. Each triad has its secular analogues, without the vitality of which there could be no health at all in our daily affairs. Patience seeks to emulate the ways of God, humility knows the infinite qualitative difference that dashes every hope of imitation, and gratitude rejoices at the divine assistance that renders possible a more than human likeness. There is only a single proper motivation for the life of discipleship, and that is gratitude. True love for God is disinterested, in the sense that it seeks nothing beyond the capacity to respond to the gifts it has been given and to the presence of the Giver. It does not seek to use God for its own purposes. Yet such responsiveness is quite beyond all our talents and powers. So we must be grateful not only for what we have received but equally for our capacity to reciprocate in faith, hope, and love, for these are also gifts and not achievements. Means and ends both elicit our gratitude: the redemption freely offered, as well as its power to transform the stoniness of the heart in a responsiveness that is our own act and yet not ours at all.

The centrality of gratitude for the Christian life, which asks for nothing except the presence of the Lord because in that companionship it possesses all things, is conveyed with singular beauty and power in anonymous seventeenth-century Latin

verses that were translated by Edward Caswell and became a Lenten hymn two centuries later:

My God, I love thee; not because
  I hope for heaven thereby,
Nor yet because who love thee not
  Are lost eternally.

Thou, O my Jesus, thou didst me
  Upon the Cross embrace;
For me didst bear the nails and spear,
  And manifold disgrace....

Then why, O blessed Jesus Christ,
  Should I not love thee well,
Not for the sake of winning heaven,
  Or of escaping hell;

Not with the hope of gaining aught,
  Not seeking a reward;
But as thyself hast loved me,
  O ever-loving Lord.[6]

As the hymn affirms, it is the love displayed in the cross of Christ that kindles in us a grateful love in return, but gratitude thus inspired inevitably grows more inclusive. We are grateful for the gift of life itself, for time and room of our own, for the restoration of community and its increase, for release from bondage to the past and to endless recriminations, for all the beauties of earth and sky and sea, for the little surprises and marvels that ornament the tapestry of daily life, for relief from the burden of self-seriousness that was inescapable when we believed that in the end we were all alone.

Why is it not only better but so much easier to give than to receive? Giving can be an act of benevolence and generosity, of course, while our readiness to grab whatever is within reach can be a disclosure of greed and anxiety about tomorrow. But why is it *easier* for us to give, if unrestrained appetites and lust are the marks of our alienation from God? Part of the answer is that giving means others are obligated to us; receiving indicates that we are under obligations to others, no matter how sincerely they protest to the contrary. Initiative and choice rest with the giver as the master of the situation, the dominant partner, and its continuation depends upon the giver's will. The recipient is a patient, involved in a situation that is not of his or her own devising. The recipient is indebted to others, no longer alone with the illusions of independence and self-sufficiency. Pride chafes at being the satellite of a larger planet, as though one were a child again. It cannot hear Jesus' words, "Unless you change and become like children..." (Matthew 18:3).

The traditional socioeconomic role of man as the breadwinner can be an expression of pride and the domination of others. Economic insecurity and the loss of employment brings more bitter anguish because of the threats they pose to the sense of identity of men who define themselves above all as breadwinners, whose notions of masculinity are bound up indissolubly with the capacity to give, and whose view of selfhood is threatened by ideas of gratitude and indebtedness, obligation and dependence. Reason for gratitude can be either a burden or an opportunity, a source of resentment or of pleasure, because gratitude enforces humility and acknowledges that we are patients in a shared world and not the solitary architects of our own.

The great occasion for gratitude in the liturgical year is Christmas. The irony of Christmas is that we who once gave gifts in humble emulation of God now often give them in order

to maintain our prideful similitude to God. We lavish more on others than they can give to us in order to reassert that we are the true centers of the worlds they inhabit; love comes all untethered from humility. But it is not always so, not for those who know the gospel is a scandal to the unregenerate heart precisely because at first it requires no sacrifice from us, just silence and acceptance, humility and gratitude, the willingness to do nothing, the willingness to be served. What could seem greater folly to all those who believe that busyness is the cure for every affliction and the typical expression of human satisfaction? What Christmas is intended to teach us is not so much to give gifts as to give thanks, which is the greatest gift. Even more important than the patient waiting that Advent enjoins is the willingness to be waited upon, and to accept it with humility and thanksgiving.

Epilogue

The Relevance of the Past

patience and the kingdom of God

There can be little doubt of the importance of the idea of patience in the Christian tradition, the extent of its neglect today, or the need for its recovery for tomorrow. Nor can we deny that our day provides an infertile and inhospitable context for its cultivation. When the values of mutuality, reciprocity, and responsiveness cease to figure in our models of what it means to be a person, the virtue of patience becomes problematical. Notions of individualism and autonomy, of an atomistic society which understands itself as no more than a collection of separate entities, of the self as its own creator and freedom as a birthright upon which there are no constraints—all these imply that patience in most of its forms inhibits rather than enriches our existence.

Patience is perhaps the best of all synonyms for the way of the Christ. But the suffering at Calvary reflects also the

everlasting richness of God's trinitarian life, the mutuality of Father and Son revealed in and through the Spirit, and the joyful suffering that love always and everywhere entails in heaven as on earth. It is not too much to say that the perfection of divine as well as human agency requires dialogical existence because the varieties of our passibility, our capacity to be affected, are as complex and enriching as our diverse activities. The doctrine of the Trinity affirms that the status of patient is essential to the perfection of divine activity. That is why no unitarian notion of God is adequate to express the inexhaustible richness and completeness of divine power. All of those who have found a social analogy useful for approaching the mystery of the divine life, such as the great Cappadocian fathers of the fourth century, have recognized that the suffering which companionship involves is at the heart of divine omnipotence. When Hilary of Poitiers, their contemporary in the West, applied the idea of coinherence to the Trinity, his intent was to emphasize both the perfect mutuality of Father, Son, and Spirit in all divine actions toward the world and within the divine life itself.

The doctrine of providence has been consistently understood within the Christian tradition as a principal justification for the virtue of patience. When its proper foundation in the life and death of Jesus Christ is no longer the center of attention, however, the doctrine is reduced to a theory of divine rule rather than a statement of God's participation in all the darkness and tension and struggle of human history. If we cannot understand patience as a divine perfection and God as himself a patient, then we can no longer find room for true mutuality and reciprocity between the Creator and the creature. Instead, the mystery of the divine-human relationship, with its diverse opportunities for finite creativity, dwindles to the problem of the just and the

unjust, the gap between what we deserve and what we suffer. Why do the wicked flourish like the green bay tree?

Perhaps the greatest loss is that we can no longer understand impatience as an element in the Christian life. If providence is merely about God's sovereignty and our submission to God's rule, then Christian patience is open to the charge of quietism. It leaves no room for the sort of impatience that is patience's own proper offspring. What if impatience is not a challenge to God's rule, but a faithful participation with God in the struggle to realize the kingdom? It is patience alone that possesses the wisdom to know when impatience is an act of discipleship and when it is not. When patience loses its connection with the possibility of impatience, its Christian character is jeopardized because it threatens to fall out of its relationship to justice and love.

Suffering can be reason for thanksgiving, for it can call us to ourselves, cause us to be accountable, teach us what is important and what is not, and persuade us to repent. Because we are not only agents but patients, we can and must cultivate patience, the primary meanings of which—enduring with equanimity, waiting calmly and expectantly, forbearance, and perseverance—are united by the attentiveness and caring they all display. As a theological virtue, patience always finds its exemplar in Jesus Christ: it is self-denial, bearing the cross, dying away from this world, participation in the sufferings of the Son of God, unbloody martyrdom, keeping silence before God. It is an activity that requires all our resources and, beyond them, the gift of God's grace. Certainly it is demanded by any form of belief in providence and any sort of hope in the eschatological promises of the gospel.

The argument of the last three chapters has been that there are theological, anthropological, and societal reasons, firmly grounded in our biological condition, to insist that patience is

necessary for human life to progress beyond childishness toward real freedom and a mature sense of responsibility. Unless we are willing to wait our turn, to display a modicum of courtesy toward those with whom we must cooperate, to accept delays and disappointments and still persevere in our daily duties, the fabric of our common life unravels to the point that it is impossible to plan for tomorrow or even sustain an extended conversation. Incivility is not a superficial problem, but a disclosure that the foundations are eroding away.

Patience is simply the embrace of what we are. We are patients, whether we like it or not; we cannot escape our own nature. We come into the world as patients and we leave it as patients, but even in our days of greatest strength our condition is no different. We cannot escape our involvements with others; nor can we seek always to be the dominant partner, for then we will have thrown away all the riches that others can offer us. Freedom is a gift from others, who give it specificity and concreteness, providing us with the human face of providence. To be human, therefore, is to be a sufferer; it is through our passibility, our capacity to be affected, that we discover our finest opportunities for agency, inventiveness, and fulfillment.

Patience and humility and gratitude together are committed to offering to all others what God has ungrudgingly given to us: the time and space they must have for their own flourishing. Patience provides the essential support so that we may live as if the new age had come. Patience means living against appearances. This is one way, and perhaps the most important way of all, to express a fundamental form of the New Testament ethical imperative—the injunction to live as if the new age had come in fullness and power, and as if this present age were no longer with us but had passed entirely away. How better to honor the biblical invitation to live "as if…as if not" than to contend against appearances by practicing the Christian

patience that forbears, perseveres, endures, and waits expectantly despite everything that pronounces this is futility and folly?

Never has the vision that supports this imperative been more beautifully expressed than in Isaiah's prophecy of a day when

> The wilderness and the dry land shall be glad,
> the desert shall rejoice and blossom;
> like the crocus it shall blossom abundantly,
> and rejoice with joy and singing....
> For waters shall break forth in the wilderness,
> and streams in the desert;
> the burning sand shall become a pool,
> and the thirsty ground springs of water.
> (Isaiah 35:1-2, 6-7)

There are other visions of the future, however, and some of them portray the coming of darkness instead of the advent of dawn, the threat of destruction rather than the promise of a new creation. In the nineteenth century the poet Shelley wrote of another desert, one that Isaiah never knew, where the traveler finds only the rubble of broken dreams, telling that all is vanity and futility. On a plinth from which its statue has long since fallen, he deciphers an inscription that boasts:

> "My name is Ozymandias, King of Kings:
> Look on my works, ye Mighty, and despair!"
> Nothing beside remains. Round the decay
> Of that colossal wreck, boundless and bare,
> The lone and level sands stretch far away.[1]

There are two cities, one shaped by the love of power and one by the power of love, one intent on domination and one on obedience, one centered upon the creature and one dedicated

to the Creator, one reclaimed by the desert and one able to make a garden there. Such creativity is more than a human enterprise, but our patience and humility and gratitude have their roles to play, and we can offer nothing better.

Afterword

Leadership and Unnatural Virtues: George Washington and the Patience of Power

by David Hein
Hood College
Frederick, Maryland

Leadership and Unnatural Virtues

Patience: How We Wait Upon the World, by David Harned, is a rich exploration of the history, meaning, and significance of a virtue that, as the author suggests, bears an intriguing relationship to power: "There are two cities, one shaped by the power of love and one by the love of power, one intent on domination and the other on obedience. . ." (183). The city of God—the community shaped by love and intent on obedience—is composed of those bound together by self-less love. This form of love, a response by creatures to the

love bestowed upon them, is distinguished and strengthened by the golden thread of patience—receptivity to the needs and gifts of others—which runs through unselfish love from top to bottom.

Yes, there are two cities, but, for Saint Augustine, they will not be separated and made manifest until the dawning of the new age that Harned writes about. Until then, we have the present age, in which power is necessary and patience a good, but in which waiting and clout, if they meet at all, have a relationship that is often wary and distant. Most ordinary citizens would probably agree that one of the chief everyday benefits of being immensely powerful must be not ever having to wait: Your motorcade will get you to that important political fundraiser sans impediment of traffic lights or beltway congestion. A staff aide can hang on the phone with the medical insurance company or the Internal Revenue Service to straighten out the problem which arrived in this morning's post with your name on it, knocking your plans sideways—or would have done if you were helpless and had to deal with these faceless clerks yourself.

Even for ordinary citizens, however, reason for hope exists on the leadership front, at least in the professional literature: power and the virtues have entered an era of rapprochement.[1] All recent studies of men and women who hold sway over others have stressed the key virtues—the positive character

1. The qualification—"at least. . ."—is important. In his review of a book by a well-known and largely successful corporate leader, Daniel Akst observes that ours may be a time of inadequate leaders, notwithstanding what he calls "the burgeoning leadership industry," which encompasses books, seminars, and conferences. "In the realm of business," he notes, "modern leaders have invited criticism thanks to their infatuation with short-term profits and their shameless embrace of staggeringly high compensation." Akst points out what "appears to be an inverse correlation between the growth of the leadership industry and the quality of the leaders we've seen in business as well as in public life." He urges would-be leaders to read books about individuals who "have grappled with the challenges and ordeals of guiding an army, a nation or a daring enterprise." Daniel Akst, "Business Bromides," review of *The Virgin Way*, by Richard Branson, *Wall Street Journal*, September 9, 2014, A15.

traits—that true leaders must possess; and selfish striving—heedless self-assertion, blinkered devotion to power or profit alone—is not among them. Often these books speak of the crucial *habits* of highly effective leaders, which is an appropriate word to use, for a virtue, according to one authoritative source, is "a habitual, well-established readiness or disposition of [a human being]'s powers directing them to some specific goodness of act."[2]

The most useful versions of the current leadership guides not only present the relevant virtues in abstract terms but also provide interesting and often familiar examples from history to shore up readers' awareness of a virtue's key features and to prompt further reflection on a virtue's connections to real-life situations and problems. Thus, for example, in their popular textbook *10 Virtues of Outstanding Leaders: Leadership and Character*, Al Gini and Ronald M. Green—academics who specialize in ethics and leadership—offer a book with two parts.

The first part discusses the virtues that characterize good leadership—although these two authors would reject the adjective "good" as unnecessary: leadership without integrity they call "misleadership," while ethical leadership is simply "leadership." They cite ten virtues as particularly important: deep honesty, moral courage, moral vision, compassion and care, fairness, intellectual excellence, creative thinking, aesthetic sensitivity, good timing, and deep selflessness.[3] Then, in their book's second part, Gini and Green offer a range of examples that illustrate their themes and engage students' interest: not surprisingly, Abraham Lincoln's moral courage and Charles de Gaulle's good timing; but also, less predictably, the authors give us Herb Kelleher and the people

2. *New Catholic Encyclopedia* (1967), s.v. "virtue." Hereafter cited as *NCE*.

3. Al Gini and Ronald M. Green, *10 Virtues of Outstanding Leaders: Leadership and Character* (Malden, MA: Wiley-Blackwell, 2013), 47–69.

of Southwest Airlines for creative thinking and Steve Jobs for aesthetic sensitivity.[4]

In other words, Gini and Green are representative of authors of leadership studies who attempt to provide their readers with concrete examples of real-life figures who were particularly good at *x*, where *x* = an outstanding trait or capacity that was right at the time for both the leader and his or her larger concern, whether that enterprise was nation or corporation, daytime talk show or struggle for civil rights. Moreover—the implication is—this particular virtue, embodied and enacted in difficult circumstances, is one that the rest of us would do well to understand, appreciate, and, possibly, adopt and adapt within our own spheres of activity.

In these case studies of effective leadership, the examples proffered are invariably individuals who have achieved excellence. Born with artistic, intellectual, athletic, creative, martial, or entrepreneurial potential, over time they have honed their skills, upped their games, and achieved a consistency of character and performance which enables them to be truly eminent within some worthwhile activity. By the time they arrive on the scene of these studies, each of them possesses, any reader would agree, a good habit that they have mastered, that has become ingrained, that appears to come—like a champion's golf stroke—with ease: "She's just a natural!"

In general usage, "natural" can mean seemingly innate—as if you were born with this skill. An action is accomplished without mannerism, without pretending or showing off or forcing it. "Natural" means *at ease*—without undue pain, anxiety, or discomfort: a natural smile. Conversely, "unnatural" can mean affected, strange, *strained*: an unnatural smile.[5]

4. Gini and Green, *10 Virtues*, chaps. 7, 12–14.

5. Moral theologians have designated some good habits as "natural virtues," human achievements that do not require an infusion of divine grace to be realized. Thereby these ethicists mean to distinguish the natural or cardinal virtues—prudence,

For all of us, some practices come more naturally than other activities, and some skills never come at all, no matter how much time we spend trying to obtain them. Gini and Green give their readers examples of leaders aligned with one outstanding trait each. A reader will observe, however, what is apparent in absence: Like us, all the greatest leaders have had many skills they could not master. Interesting problems appear when in crucial moments these leaders lack but nonetheless need skills that have not become natural to them. What happens in the careers of key figures when leadership requires excellence in their unnatural virtues?

Sometimes, granted, this problem scarcely arises. In the heyday of the civil rights movement, the cause of social justice received what it needed in leadership and attendant virtues: the faith and hope of Fannie Lou Hamer, the courage and dignity-with-justice of Rosa Parks, the prudence and perseverance of Martin Luther King.[6]

But many times, when leaders require the right virtues in the right combinations at the right time, the result is decidedly problematic. For example, in September 1862 General George C. McClellan at Sharpsburg, Maryland: temperance, no question, but fortitude? Or General R. E. Lee on the third day of

fortitude, temperance, and justice—from the theological virtues of faith, hope, and love. This differentiation, whatever assistance it might provide in focusing our attention on the distinctive qualities of those habitual inclinations that concern life in relation to God (the theological virtues), is problematic in other respects, as well as being rigid, confusing, and counter to ordinary human experience. In fact, in an earlier book, Harned provides a discussion of this distinction between the so-called natural and theological virtues which makes quite clear, by way of insights and examples rooted in common life, why this formal demarcation should be approached with caution. *Faith and Virtue* (Philadelphia: Pilgrim, 1973), 16–17, 32, 34, 35, 125, 144–49, 174. For an alternative view, see Robert Sokolowski, *The God of Faith and Reason* (Notre Dame, IN: University of Notre Dame Press, 1982), 53–87.

6. For brief but useful discussions of Rosa Parks and Fannie Lou Hamer, see Bruce J. Dierenfield and John White, *A History of African-American Leadership*, 3rd ed. (Harlow, UK: Pearson, 2012), 129–31, 217–23.

the battle of Gettysburg, at the moment when, in the novelist William Faulkner's well-known words, it's "not yet two oclock on that July afternoon in 1863 . . . and Pickett himself with his long oiled ringlets and his hat in one hand probably and his sword in the other looking up the hill waiting for Longstreet to give the word and it's all in the balance": Their commander did not lack courage, Generals Longstreet and Pickett would have acknowledged to one another, but did prudence forsake General Lee?[7]

Or, in the Second World War and its immediate aftermath, General George S. Patton: brains for tactics and guts for glory—famously—but human compassion and astute political judgment? How much greater—as men and leaders—might both British Field Marshal Bernard Law Montgomery and U.S. General Mark Clark have been if they had only possessed a little more humility? Patton and tact, McClellan and boldness, or Douglas MacArthur and modesty: regrettably, in each case, a powerful man and a requisite virtue at arm's length from each other.

This point about unnatural virtues is not novel. The *New Catholic Encyclopedia* notes that "inbred characteristics of temperament, even of body, may favor the development of virtue"—or not favor the development of one or more particular virtues.[8] And anyone can see that faith, hope, and love stand a better chance of taking root and flourishing in a child whose family life is stable and not plagued by abuse or neglect.

More than two hundred years ago, the evangelical Anglican Hannah More, who was both a writer and a prominent leader in the education field, noticed moral discrepancies among individuals and offered fitting words of counsel: If we really want to improve, then "we should cultivate most assiduously,

7. William Faulkner, *Intruder in the Dust* (New York: Random House, 1948), 194.

8. *NCE*, s.v. "virtue."

because the work is so difficult, those graces which are most opposite to our natural temper." The strength "of our good qualities," she knew, depends "much on their being produced by the victory over some natural wrong propensity." More remarked that "the implantation of a virtue is the eradication of a vice." Thus, she astutely observed, "it will cost one man more to keep down a rising passion than to do a brilliant deed." Another person will have more trouble holding "back a sparkling but corrupt thought . . . than he would to give a large sum in charity."[9] Why? Because for this last fellow, for whatever reason in his personal formation, generosity is a natural virtue, while patience—which bids him wait and attend to the contributions of others instead of horning in with his own clever, cutting comments—is an unnatural virtue. Thus this person will have to work hard to cultivate forbearance, chiefly by checking his thrusting ego.

This impetuous man's unnatural virtue, patience, appears to be especially variable in its distribution. To find remarkable case studies, I need look no farther than the backyard of my own family history. My mother—by nature or nurture, by choice or calling—was patient to the point of saintliness. To the same degree, my father was congenitally impatient, habitually hyperkinetic—save when his sons needed him most, and then all his peripheral projects came to a standstill.

For Mother Teresa, patience appears to have been a natural virtue. For the protofeminist Mary Wollstonecraft, on the other hand, practicing patience—in relation to her immediate circumstances or to society at large—would have been a struggle: her father squandered the fortune he inherited, failed at farming, took to the bottle, bullied his wife, rambled about, and fell lower at each move. After their mother's death, Mary

9. Hannah More, *Practical Piety* (Burlington, NJ: D. Allinson, 1811), 30.

and her two sisters found living in their father's house intolerable, and as soon they were able they left home for good.[10]

Not so surprisingly, Mary Wollstonecraft rather impatiently decided to delineate patience as one of "the negative virtues" expected of women, along with docility and other traits "incompatible with any exertion of intellect."[11] An excessively narrow view of the possibilities of patience, at least as represented by the word "waiting," comes through, also, in some phrasing in the essayist Joseph Epstein's account of his friend Erich Heller, who had "genuinely elegant manners." Courteous and humane, Heller, Epstein recalls, was "a good listener, which is rare for a professor (among professors, a wag once remarked, there is no listening—only waiting)."[12]

We nod appreciatively at this parenthetical distinction because we catch the opposition between two gerunds that, in another context, could be synonyms. The humor in this wag's remark hinges on an emaciated construction of waiting—a usage altogether different from what Harned in his subtitle and his mentor W. H. Vanstone in his main title mean by waiting.[13] Both these writers are keen to stress the *stature* of waiting. By "waiting," Harned and Vanstone mean patience, and they intend to construe and commend patience in its most full-blooded form. In brief, they understand "waiting" to signify the same *disponibilité d'esprit* which in Epstein's verbal miniature is signified by "listening": receptivity to the initiative of the other, attentiveness, not straining against ennui, mentally drumming one's fingers, and reluctantly biding one's time until

10. *Dictionary of National Biography* (1950), s.v. "Godwin, Mrs. Mary Wollstonecraft."

11. Mary Wollstonecraft, *A Vindication of the Rights of Woman, with Strictures on Political and Moral Subjects*, ed. Charles W. Hagelman Jr. (1792; New York: Norton, 1967), 101.

12. Joseph Epstein, *Essays in Biography* (Mount Jackson, VA: Axios, 2012), 507.

13. W. H. Vanstone, *The Stature of Waiting* (London: Darton, Longman & Todd, 1982).

the opportunity at last presents itself to pontificate on some rarefied subject or to pounce with another bon mot.[14] We all recognize this professional type—perhaps when we look in the mirror.

In truth, consistently living the virtues is hard for everyone. All the virtues are unnatural—a strain—to some extent and most of the time. Which is why people pray for an infusion of divine grace to empower in them even the formally designated natural, or cardinal, virtues of temperance, prudence, justice, and fortitude: "Sweet Jesus, please keep me sober today." Or the Serenity Prayer, which ends with a petition for "the wisdom to know the one [what cannot be changed] from the other [what can and ought to be changed]." And the earnest request I heard my harried dad mutter most often: "Give me strength, Lord!"

C. S. Lewis would have thought my father was on to something important. He would have recognized my dad's simple prayer as a plea for the essential requirement for doing any good at all: *fortitudo,* firm resolve in the hour of need. As Lewis says in *The Screwtape Letters,* "courage is not simply *one* of the virtues, but the form of every virtue at the testing point. . . ." Fortitude is the skeleton that enables the virtues to stand up, be strong, and do their jobs in the face of adversity. "A chastity or honesty or mercy which yields to danger," Lewis points out, "will be chaste or honest or merciful only on conditions. Pilate was merciful till it became risky."[15]

George Washington had nonpareil physical courage throughout his life, and he had moral courage when his

14. See Harned, *Patience,* 127–29, 181.

15. C. S. Lewis, *The Screwtape Letters* (1942; New York: Touchstone/Simon & Schuster, 1996), 104 (emphasis in original). On the crucial relation between fortitude and prudence, which—through the closely allied virtue of justice—tells the stout human being what is worth fighting and risking injury for, see Josef Pieper, *The Four Cardinal Virtues* (New York: Harcourt, Brace & World, 1965), 117–25; Harned, *Faith and Virtue,* 139.

country needed it. *Fortitudo* supplied the form that patience required at the testing point. A recent Washington biographer reveals a solid understanding of fortitude when he acknowledges that "endurance and fortitude may seem passive virtues, but they take a huge effort of active will." He has in mind in particular the stretch of time that commenced the week before Christmas 1777, as George Washington led his troops into Valley Forge, Pennsylvania, and established winter quarters there. From that point, the Continental Army commander and his men began a three-year experience in endurance, during which "they plumbed the meaning of waiting out the enemy."[16] As the leading authority on Washington's military record puts it in his biography of the general: "Washington was never very good at waiting, but that is how he spent the years between 1778 and 1781."[17]

George Washington and the Patience of Power

In contemporary American society, these two key terms, "patience" and "power," have been joined in the trendy phrase "the power of patience." This theme has become the subject of popular books and articles that teach calmness and the avoidance of hurry and stress: focusing on the task at hand, enjoying life in the moment, practicing mindful living. This salutary approach is reflected in the Slow Movement: slow eating, slow reading, slow travel, slow gardening, even slow church.

George Washington would come to know the power of patience, but the more valuable lesson to take from his life and career is the deep worth of the patience of power. Although he

16. Myron Magnet, *The Founders at Home: The Building of America, 1735–1817* (New York: Norton, 2014), 154. On patience as a constituent of moral courage, see Harned, *Faith and Virtue*, 142.

17. Edward G. Lengel, *General George Washington: A Military Life* (New York: Random House, 2005), 307.

may not be widely recognized as such today, Washington was the most consequential leader—and the greatest president—in the history of the United States of America.[18] Most of us are capable of practicing patience, and we often have to, but we hold little power. George Washington, on the other hand, had little innate patience but held immense power. He was thoroughly familiar with the uses of power, including its potential for both benefit and harm.[19] As Edmund S. Morgan has stated, "Washington's genius lay in his understanding of power, both military power and political power, an understanding unmatched by that of any of his contemporaries."[20]

Among Washington's leading unnatural virtues, patience was probably foremost. He was exceedingly ambitious: avid for advancement and fame, eager to claim wealth and status. He craved control and eschewed dependency in any form.[21] Especially as a young, inexperienced officer serving the British Army, Washington could be not only courageous but also impetuous. He was, as one historian has remarked, "by natural disposition inclined to be fiery and temperamental."[22] Speaking of Washington's efforts to restrain his worst impulses, another historian says it became easy for later generations to see

18. See Peter R. Henriques, *Realistic Visionary: A Portrait of George Washington* (Charlottesville: University of Virginia Press, 2006), ix–x; Gordon S. Wood, *Revolutionary Characters: What Made the Founders Different* (New York: Penguin, 2006), 31.

19. Henriques, *Realistic Visionary*, 41, 42.

20. Edmund S. Morgan, *The Genius of George Washington* (New York: Norton, 1977), 6. Morgan goes on to affirm that just as Washington "understood the political basis of military power, so also he understood, far better than Congress did, its economic basis" (16). See Magnet, *The Founders at Home*, 162.

21. Henriques, *Realistic Visionary*, 2; Joseph J. Ellis, *His Excellency: George Washington* (New York: Vintage, 2004), 47, 51, 64.

22. Don Higginbotham, *George Washington and George Marshall: Some Reflections on the American Military Tradition*, The Harmon Memorial Lectures in Military History, no. 26 (Colorado Springs, CO: United States Air Force Academy, 1984), 12.

only the steady demeanor of the Father of Our Country and to overlook the "powerful latent forces" lurking just beneath his surface calm. Consequently, "we have forgotten the effort his self-control required. We treat what was a result as a natural condition, as if Washington had been carved from the same stone as his monument."[23]

The results of Washington's fiery temperament are well known to any student of his life: his reckless actions could lead to disaster. Such was the case in 1754, when he was a lieutenant colonel and second in command (and, after his colonel's death, fully in command) of the Virginia Regiment in engagements with the French in the region of Great Meadows, not far from present-day Uniontown, Pennsylvania.[24] One of his leading biographers provides a quick, unflattering pen portrait: "Although in moments of reflection conscious of his inadequacies, in action he could be rash, brash, impolitic, over-self-confident. He made dreadful mistakes."[25]

Looking at this same period, another historian concludes that "there is something unlikable about the George Washington of 1753–1758 [aged twenty-one to twenty-six]. He seems a trifle raw and strident, too much on his dignity, too ready to complain, too nakedly concerned with promotion." Young Washington could come across as pushy and impertinent, altogether too hungry for honor and preferment. "He had yet to learn," this biographer notes, "the wisdom of patience; or rather, he was learning it in a painful school."[26]

23. Richard Brookhiser, *Founding Father: Rediscovering George Washington* (New York: Simon & Schuster, 1997), 6; see also 116, 118–19. Directly relevant to Brookhiser's theme is the relation between patience and temperance: see Harned, *Patience*, 157–58.

24. See Lengel, *General George Washington*, 34–42.

25. James Thomas Flexner, *Washington: The Indispensable Man* (New York: Back Bay, 1974), 37. See Ellis, *His Excellency*, 12–18.

26. Marcus Cunliffe, *George Washington: Man and Monument* (New York: New

In light of Washington's habitual disposition, why not refer to his difficulties with patience by using only the words for its related vices, such as "rashness," rather than an awkward phrase and roundabout concept like "unnatural virtue"? The answer is that Washington knew that patience was a virtue: "Patience is a noble virtue," he declared, "and, when rightly exercised, does not fail of its reward."[27] And, just as he learned from experience about the military command of men in the field, so he learned about the inner command of his own wayward instincts. Over the decades, as Washington gained experience in leadership, the narrative arc of his character gradually bent down and away from unalloyed self-assertion; in him the quality of patience became less strained.

The theory of behavior that Washington and his peers knew and attempted to live by did not view any virtue as natural. What is natural, they thought, is human beings' self-interested seeking after their own success and longing for others' acclaim. People do not give unselfishly of themselves or perform heroically because they are naturally altruistic or fearless in the face of threats to their lives or social positions. By the same token, a zeal for acknowledgment of their worth—for honor—*is* innate, Washington and his contemporaries believed. While fortifying their own self-esteem is an activity that individuals gladly beaver away at, self-mastery, the seemly control and direction of *amour-propre,* is a much harder slog—and needs all the props of morality and religion that society can muster. Washington's peers knew this desire for distinction as "pride" or "emulation." A gentleman could win approval in the eyes of those he respected by manifesting a moral character and acting

American Library, 1958), 54. See Henriques, *Realistic Visionary,* chap. 1.

27. George Washington to Reverend John Rodgers, June 11, 1783, in *The Writings of George Washington,* ed. John C. Fitzpatrick, 39 vols. (Washington, DC: Government Printing Office, 1931–44), 27:1.

in a socially approved manner—and most praiseworthy of all were enterprises that served the commonweal.[28]

By these means could a person both practice a virtue such as patience and "not fail of its reward." Washington was always realistic about human motives and the power of interest; he believed that the best deeds men and women can accomplish in this world are acts that are generous but never completely free of the taint of self-regard. "Patience is a noble virtue." In time, even if Washington was under considerable strain when making the attempt, he came to exemplify his maxim, writes Douglas Southall Freeman, "and he scarcely lost patience except in dealing with three classes—cowards, those whom he believed to be of habitual rascality, and, above all, those who were cheating the American people for their own profit in the life-and-death struggle for independence."[29]

For the commander-in-chief of the Continental Army, waiting might not have come easily, but it did bring results. A military historian has summarized the positive effects of patience on the course of the American Revolution: "With [British General Henry] Clinton bottled up in New York, it was patience that brought the war to a successful conclusion: patience with dilatory French assistance; patience with an army that mutinied twice; patience with a Congress that demanded but did not provide; patience while [American General Nathanael] Greene lost the battles but won the war in the South," and, finally, to help bring about the war's rather surprising conclusion, "patience that was at last rewarded when the French navy briefly won control of the sea around Yorktown, enabling Washington to deliver the coup de grâce."[30]

28. Wood, *Revolutionary Characters*, 34–35; Magnet, *The Founders at Home*, 109.

29. Douglas Southall Freeman, *George Washington: A Biography*, 7 vols. (New York: Scribner's, 1952), 5:489. See Magnet, *The Founders at Home*, 160.

30. Hugh Bicheno, "Washington, Gen. George," in *The Oxford Companion to Military History*, ed. Richard Holmes (Oxford: Oxford University Press, 2001), 985.

At least as crucial to American victory as waiting for the right coalition of forces at the right moment was waiting's close companion in the school of virtue: perseverance. During the winter of 1777–1778 at Valley Forge, twenty miles northwest of Philadelphia, men froze and starved to death before their commander's eyes. As typhus, pneumonia, and dysentery ran through the camp, the death rate soared. Hospital care was sketchy at best, often riskier than trying to cope on one's own. For this reason, many soldiers stayed in their huts and spread their diseases throughout the camp.[31] From Valley Forge, General Washington wrote of "Men without Cloathes to cover their nakedness, without Blankets to lay on, without Shoes, by which their Marches might be traced by the Blood from their feet, and almost as often without Provisions as with. . . ."[32] His officers went home on furlough; Washington stayed in camp with his men. And the snowy, frigid winter of 1779–1780 was even worse: Continental Army soldiers encamped at Morristown, New Jersey, were reduced to eating dogs, the bark from trees, and their boots.

Through the long years of war, Washington never returned to Mount Vernon, although he thought of it continually and longed to be there. He persevered in the face of crippling supply and money problems, second-guessing by Congress, and military setbacks, such as the British capture of the American capital, Philadelphia (1777), and the fall of Charleston and the destruction of Camden, in South Carolina (1780)—defeats which made the patriot cause look uncertain in the extreme.[33]

By 1777, following the capture of Philadelphia, Washington realized that he had to be patient, for he must do whatever

31. Lengel, *General George Washington*, 269–72.

32. George Washington to John Banister, April 21, 1778, in *George Washington: Writings*, ed. John Rhodehamel (New York: Library of America, 1997), 303.

33. Joseph Ellis believes that "in the end, steadfastness was [Washington's] most valuable attribute, along with the stamina that accompanied it." *His Excellency*, 88.

was necessary not to lose the war; he had to preserve the Continental Army as a fighting force. This strategic recognition not only went against his own aggressive nature, which urged him to fight—and win, but also went against the wishes of many patriots, including critics of his military prowess. Washington, however, declined to launch an imprudent attack.[34]

In his courage and perseverance throughout the Revolution, George Washington revealed his reliance on patience—and feelingly used the word when referring to his men at Valley Forge. To George Clinton, governor of New York, he wrote: "A part of the army has been a week, without any kind of flesh, and the rest three or four days. Naked and starving as they are, we cannot enough admire the incomparable patience and fidelity of the soldiery, that they have not been ere this excited by their sufferings, to a general mutiny and dispersion."[35]

By war's end, both officers and men were aware of Washington's sacrifice, of which serving without pay was the least significant aspect. His officers' appreciation of his endurance with them of what they had suffered for the cause of independence was the only real chink in their armor during their 1783 revolt at Newburgh, New York, over not receiving their wages from Congress in the long interim between victory and peace treaty. On March 15, 1783, Washington would soften their rebellious hearts by stumbling over words in sentences his aging eyes had trouble making out and by putting on his new spectacles—his officers had never seem him wear glasses—and in that simple way remind them of all they had been through together.[36] "The disarming gesture of putting on his glasses," biographer Ron Chernow writes, "moved the officers to tears

34. Ellis, *His Excellency*, 92, 95, 97, 99, 107, 109; Lengel, *General George Washington*, 150.

35. George Washington to George Clinton, February 16, 1778, in Rhodehamel, *George Washington: Writings*, 292.

36. See Ron Chernow, *Washington: A Life* (New York: Penguin, 2010), 433–36.

as they recalled the legendary sacrifices he had made for his country. When he left the hall moments later, the threatened mutiny had ended, and his victory was complete."[37]

Perseverance as a type of patience helps to resolve questions about an apparent anomaly that appears when we hold George Washington up to the light of moral scrutiny—for patience (even as an "unnatural virtue") seems a strange virtue to claim for any fighting revolutionary. Within the effort to achieve victory once war is under way—that is, as a tactical weapon to win battles or a strategic policy to prevail in the long run over a powerful foe—waiting and endurance make sense. But is it right—specifically from the vantage point of *jus ad bellum* criteria—to call a principal actor in an armed rebellion *patient*?

Moral theologians, just-war theorists, ethically minded historians, and certainly Christian pacifists would have trouble agreeing to that designation.[38] Should not George Washington have worked with other Americans—men and women representing the full range of interest groups and social classes—to resolve issues of taxation and political representation nonviolently? Then, in good time, the contending parties might well have achieved a suitable accommodation of their differences and realized just results without bloodshed.

The issues raised are too vast for this essay, but a partial answer might invoke the similarly curious case of Job. The author of the Letter of James appears to hold up Job as a role model of suffering and patience (5:10–11). And yet even a casual observer can see that Job is not patient at all; he complains about his afflictions, proclaims his righteousness, and

37. Chernow, *Washington*, 436. See Lengel, *General George Washington*, 349.

38. For analysis by an ethically minded historian, see George Marsden, "The American Revolution: Partisanship, 'Just Wars,' and Crusades," in *The Wars of America: Christian Views*, ed. Ronald A. Wells (Grand Rapids, MI: Eerdmans, 1981), 11–24.

demands his day in court. If he was patient, then he was patient in some manner other than passively accepting his fate.

Job was indeed patient, scholars say, in the sense of perseverance; and in this way he exemplified the proper range and limits of protest as well as the obligation to be steadfast in proclaiming what is true. Job's voice, writes John Barton, an Oxford University professor of the interpretation of holy scripture, is "the voice of a man unjustly tormented, who refuses to abandon his right to complain about it." Dynamic perseverance in a cause committed to overturning injustice and to fostering true peace—we will have to set to one side the question of whether the American Revolution was a just war and simply assume that it can be fairly evaluated as such—can be an instance of patience. "Perhaps the reception of Job shows that James was not so wrong," Barton says, "if we gloss 'patience' as 'endurance' or 'persistence.'" [39] As Mark Larrimore, the author of a recent biography of the book of Job, writes: "Maybe the attitude of persistent Job, insisting on justice, is not impatience but true patience. The narrator's assurance that Job 'didn't sin with his lips' (2:10) and God's claim (twice) that Job had 'spoken of me what is right' (42:6, 7) led premodern readers to see the book of Job as demonstrating just how much a patient person *could* say without sinning."[40]

Fighting for a just cause—especially one that is alarmingly novel and transformative—will strike many people as "impatient": thus civil-right leaders were often urged to "wait."[41] But perseverance in a worthy undertaking may be one of the highest expressions of patience, where patience means being

39. John Barton, "Angry in Verse," review of *The Book of Job: A Biography*, by Mark Larrimore, *Times Literary Supplement*, March 14, 2014, 24. See Harned, *Patience*, 60.

40. Mark Larrimore, *The Book of Job: A Biography* (Princeton, NJ: Princeton University Press, 2013), 14–15 (emphasis in original).

41. See Harned, *Patience*, 2, 3, 136, 153, 156, 161, 166.

truly responsive to citizens' just claims and a willingness to go to the limit on behalf of what is right.

Josef Pieper helps to nail down this point when he removes some possible misunderstandings of what "patience" implies. He notes that patience does not mean "an indiscriminate, self-immolating, crabbed, joyless, and spineless submission to whatever evil is met with." Quite to the contrary: patience enables a person not to be done in by evil, not to be bowed down forever by sorrow and grief. It certainly does not mean automatically capitulating to the way things happen to be and surrendering to a terrible status quo. "Patience does not imply the exclusion of energetic, forceful activity. . . . Patience keeps man from the danger that his spirit may be broken by grief and lose its greatness." For example, godly patience would never counsel an abused woman to sit there and take it; for patience, as Pieper makes clear, is completely on the side of preserving the "ultimate integrity" of the human person.[42]

This discussion of perseverance provides a valuable backdrop to consideration of a form of patience emphasized by Harned which is particularly intriguing in its relation to power: handing over.[43] Indeed, in their treatments of this topic in biographies of Washington, most writers do not use the word "patience" at all. Thus it is one of the notable contributions of Harned's work to alert us to this dimension of the virtue, for this facet of patience can reflect light on the most significant episodes of Washington's career.

Surrendering power—resigning as commander-in-chief of the Continental Army on December 23, 1783—was an act astonishing to many because so unnatural: everyone knew that great victors' thirst for power was unquenchable. As historians have pointed out, that assumption was based on the evidence of two thousand years of world history. In his

42. Pieper, *The Four Cardinal Virtues,* 129. See Harned, *Patience,* 133.

43. See Vanstone, *The Stature of Waiting,* 94.

discussion of this event at the end of a conservative revolution, historian Gordon S. Wood draws attention to its dramatic features: "Washington, consummate actor that he was, made his most theatrical gesture, his most moral mark, and the results were monumental." This resignation, "the greatest act of his life," made him "internationally famous." By handing over his sword to Congress and retiring to Mount Vernon, he "stunned the world." Its reverberations were felt throughout Europe. "It was extraordinary; a victorious general's surrendering his arms and returning to his farm was unprecedented in modern times. Cromwell, William of Orange, Marlborough—all had sought political rewards commensurate with their military achievements." Washington, many believed, could have become king or autocrat, but he refused the opportunity. "He was sincere in his desire for all his soldiers to return home," and people took him at his word. His resignation "filled them with awe." King George III said that if Washington followed through on his promise and retired to his farm, then he would be "the greatest man in the world." In 1784 Thomas Jefferson indicated that Washington's virtuous act of relinquishment likely prevented the Revolution from being seized by firebrands and its liberal goals perverted into ends radically different. Through his dramatic gesture, Wood writes, Washington became "a living embodiment of all the classical republican virtue the age was eagerly striving to recover."[44]

His decision to retire to Mount Vernon meant that, as Garry Wills states the paradoxical achievement, George Washington "gained power from his readiness to give it up." And Wills goes on to elucidate the nub of Jefferson's concern: "in accepting the ideal of Cincinnatus, Washington automatically limited the dangers of charismatic leadership, which is always at least quasi-religious, an assertion of semi-divine 'grace.'"[45]

44. Wood, *Revolutionary Characters*, 41, 42.

45. *Cincinnatus: George Washington and the Enlightenment* (Garden City, NY:

What enabled Washington to be so different from other victorious commanders? How—and where—did he learn patience? One answer highlights his growth in the small virtues of social etiquette: learning the basic courtesies of giving heed to others. A historian points out that "his statesmanship"—including his refusal to become an American Caesar—"evolved from codes of conduct and self-scrutiny he began developing as a young man."[46] Although his father died when he was only eleven and his mother consistently withheld her approval, George Washington "refused to yield to self-pity, and devising a regimen of self-improvement that was at once moral and practical, he mastered the maxims of 'genteel' etiquette even as he taught himself the practical art of land surveying."[47] As he matured, Washington became willing to attend to the views of those better informed than he, to weigh their opinions, and often to adjust his ideas accordingly.[48]

Other forces probably contributed to his patience, as well. Surviving deadly illnesses and armed attacks, discovering as a young officer that aggressiveness alone did not yield favorable results, receiving remarkable opportunities following the deaths of others, caring for his extended family at Mount Vernon, tending his fields and raising crops, reading encouragements to equanimity and gratitude in philosophical and religious texts, identifying with a national cause and subordinating his personal aggressive instincts to a goal that required a defensive strategy—all these experiences undoubtedly

Doubleday, 1984), 23.

46. Michael Knox Beran, "The Private Faces of Public Virtue," review of *The Founders at Home: The Building of America, 1735–1817*, by Myron Magnet, *Claremont Review of Books*, Summer 2014, 63.

47. Beran, "The Private Faces," 64.

48. John R. Alden, *George Washington: A Biography* (Baton Rouge: Louisiana State University Press, 1984), 90.

taught Washington various aspects of the virtue of patience.[49] He believed in a benevolent Providence who looked out for him and for his country. And certainly toward the end of his public career, in his own presidential administration, he saw and lamented the consequences of intemperate self-assertion by Alexander Hamilton and Thomas Jefferson. He told the latter that "his earnest wish" and "fondest hope" were that "instead of wounding suspicions and irritable charges," there might be "liberal allowances," "mutual forbearances," and "temporising yieldings on *all sides*"; in other words, replace rancor with patience.[50]

Moreover, Washington's response to the patriot cause—his republican turn—effected modifications in his conceptions of honor, power, and patience, as well as in his view of slavery.[51] Addressing the historical conundrum of what caused such first-class leadership as the Founding Fathers represented to arise in a nation with a white population of fewer than three million souls, Henry Steele Commager pointed to the urgent, inviting opportunities present in the public arena in the 1770s and 1780s. Washington's generation had to win independence, set up state governments, write a federal constitution, and make their new government succeed. These challenges summoned character and resourcefulness. Dramatically new occasions brought new duties, which called for fresh understandings of power and virtue.[52]

Never a saint, Washington was a man whose intense desire for honor dovetailed with the American people's need for

49. See Vanstone, *The Stature of Waiting*, 35; Brookhiser, *Founding Father*, 121–36; Ellis, *His Excellency*, 109.

50. George Washington, "To Thomas Jefferson," August 23, 1792, in Rhodehamel, *George Washington: Writings*, 817 (emphasis in original).

51. Wood, *Revolutionary Characters*, 37–41.

52. Henry Steele Commager, "Leadership in Eighteenth-Century America and Today," *Daedalus* 90, no. 4 (1961) 655.

leadership. During the quest for independence, as Washington responded to the meaning of the Revolution, he became more republican and egalitarian in his apprehension of honor.[53] "By Yorktown," writes Alan Pell Crawford, "Washington seemed less the Old World patrician than New World democrat, as he relied increasingly on the sound judgment and native ingenuity of men such as Henry Knox."[54] A school dropout, Knox was a devoted student of military history who impressed Washington not with his professional experience—for he was a bookseller, not an army officer—or his place in the social hierarchy, but with his energy, commitment, and resourcefulness. Washington put him in command of the artillery of the Continental Army, where Knox performed responsibly and well. He and Nathanael Greene—who began his education in military tactics by reading manuals from Henry Knox's bookshop—became their commander's favorite generals.[55]

The larger cause of liberty not only transformed Washington's understanding of honor; it also reduced his assessment of the value of possessing authority not granted by the people. What was important was what this dangerous instrument, power, was used for, who wielded it, and whether it was in accord with the consent of the governed. Attending to the demands of this nascent republic, with its new political realities, required patience in all its forms. As Harned says in this book, "Patience is a civic virtue." In society at large, "there can be no representative government without the patience that sustains an electoral process" (17; see also 113).

53. Beran, "The Private Faces," 64. See David Hackett Fischer, *Washington's Crossing* (New York: Oxford University Press, 2004), 273; Lengel, *General George Washington*, 196; Chernow, *Washington: A Life*, 196.

54. Alan Pell Crawford, "A Few Men of Character," review of *George Washington: Gentleman Warrior*, by Stephen Brumwell, and *Sons of the Father*, by Robert M. S. McDonald, *Wall Street Journal*, December 10, 2013, A17.

55. Lengel, *General George Washington*, xxviii; Magnet, *The Founders at Home*, 139.

And in a republic, leaders must accommodate themselves to what Harned, following Kierkegaard, refers to as "the slowness of the good" (100). Edmund S. Morgan describes the development of Washington's "remarkable" ability to tolerate temporary problems while waiting for the people first to feel the wrong that needs fixing and then to discern the best way forward. Morgan praises Washington's "patience in waiting for the people to do the right thing."[56]

During the Revolution, despite endless frustrations with obtaining needed resources from Congress, Washington remained patient. Morgan writes: "Although Washington's complaints to Congress were fruitless, he never appealed over the heads of Congress to their constituents"—for two reasons. First, he did not want the British to know the true condition of the Continental Army—"when the only thing between him and defeat was the fact that the enemy did not realize how weak he was." Second, his forbearance in working with elected representatives was directly linked to his republican virtue: "In spite of the imperious manner in which he bolstered his ability to command, Washington was a republican. He had been fully persuaded that the king of England and the minions surrounding him were conspiring to destroy the liberties of Americans." Therefore he accepted that the "principles of republican liberty" required that the military "be forever subordinate to the civil power." Congress and the state governments might be short-sighted and stingy, but Washington "never even suggested that he and his army should be anything but their servants." He could have raised a large popular following on his own and commanded troops "in defiance of the do-nothing congress"—and his officers and men would have supported him. "But he accepted the premises of republican government as an Oliver Cromwell never did." Even if he had to submit to "a body that became increasingly incompetent, irresponsible,

56. Morgan, *The Genius*, 14.

and corrupt, he never sought power on any other terms than those on which he had initially accepted it, as servant of the people." Therefore he stood against all threats—whether mutinies by the men or revolts by his officers—to undermine the civil authority; and, in the end, he willingly handed over the power entrusted to him.[57]

Another possible influence on Washington's commitment to patience is one that is easily overlooked, especially in the context of "handing over." Although he almost never referred to Jesus in his written statements, in his "Circular to State Governments" (1783), Washington did mention him as a pattern. Composed in the last months of the Revolution, this message incorporated Washington's "earnest prayer . . . that God would . . . incline the hearts of the Citizens . . . to entertain a brotherly affection and love for one another . . . and to demean ourselves with that Charity, humility and pacific temper of mind, which were the Characteristicks of the Divine Author of our blessed Religion, and without an humble imitation of whose example in these things, we can never hope to be a happy Nation."[58] "Charity, humility and pacific temper of mind" embraced in imitation of Jesus and exercised in relation to others are three moral habits that effectively circumscribe the substance of the virtue of patience.

Throughout his life, a fairly regular—although by no means an every-Sunday—participant in divine worship, Washington was apparently not an orthodox Trinitarian believer (although he was so reserved about personal matters that

57. Morgan, *The Genius*, 12–13.

58. George Washington, "Circular to State Governments," June 8, 1783, in Rhodehamel, *George Washington: Writings*, 526. See Mary V. Thompson, *"In the Hands of a Good Providence": Religion in the Life of George Washington* (Charlottesville: University of Virginia Press, 2008), 102–3; Michael Novak and Jana Novak, *Washington's God: Religion, Liberty, and the Father of Our Country* (New York: Basic, 2006), 156–58; and Brookhiser, *Founding Father*, 147–48.

no one knows for sure).[59] But even if he was a Latitudinarian Anglican, an Enlightenment Christian, or a conservative Deist, he would have viewed Jesus as—at least—an exemplar of virtue. In the published circular just quoted, he goes farther, of course, and refers to Jesus as "the Divine Author of our blessed Religion." Whenever he was in church, Washington could not have failed to be aware of the core elements of the narrative of Jesus Christ. Described not only in hymns and prayers and creeds, in scripture readings and sermons, but also in visible symbols, the patience of Christ was everywhere exhibited.

As a soldier or statesman more absorbed by the moral behavior enjoined by religion or philosophy than by metaphysical doctrine or sacred ritual, Washington would have attended to the lineaments of Jesus' life. As David Harned makes clear in *Patience*, Jesus' story features the central paradox of handing over and thereby realizing his destiny. And his followers' vocational truth is expressed in a related paradox: patient service yields perfect freedom.[60] As Harned writes, "Paradoxical as it may seem, self-denial can provide us with unexpected strength that otherwise we never could have found for ourselves" (86).

For George Washington, his stature and his standing down were two sides of the same coin of character and command. He achieved nobility in the way he responded to the initiatives—and the yearnings—of his countrymen; their patriotic hopes drew out the best in him. The paradigm of the "Divine Author" of his religion may have influenced him, as well. In his lifetime at least, Washington the man did not become a mere monument; he remained, almost literally, too grounded in the soil of his beloved Mount Vernon to let that happen.[61] Thus

59. See David L. Holmes, *The Faiths of the Founding Fathers* (New York: Oxford University Press, 2006), chap. 6; Magnet, *The Founders at Home*, 208–9.

60. See Harned, *Patience*, 39.

61. See Magnet, *The Founders at Home*, chaps. 3–5; Wood, *Revolutionary Characters*, 34. In his last will and testament, George Washington divided Mount Vernon

he never became completely alienated into his role as general or president; he preserved his integrity as a person. In George Washington's leadership as well as in its lasting benefits, we can appreciate the good fruits of the patience of power.

into five separate plots with different heirs, thereby precluding the possibility of a dynasty. And he made provisions to free the slaves that he owned and to provide funds to care for very young freed slaves as well as the old and infirm. Joseph Ellis sees Washington's will as "his ultimate exit statement, a wholly personal expression of his willingness to surrender power in a truly final fashion as he prepared to depart the stage of life itself." *His Excellency*, 265.

Notes

CHAPTER ONE

1. William F. Lynch, SJ, *Images of Hope* (Baltimore: Helicon Press, 1965), 177.
2. W. H. Vanstone, *The Stature of Waiting* (London: Darton, Longman and Todd, 1982), 50, 110.
3. *Ibid.*, 50.
4. Josef Pieper, *Leisure: The Basis of Culture*, Alexander Dru, trans. (London: Faber & Faber, 1952), 51-52.
5. *Ibid.*, 75.
6. *Ibid.*, 48-49.
7. *Ibid.*, 42.
8. Vanstone, *Stature of Waiting*, 111.
9. *Ibid.*, 112.
10. An invaluable resource for the study of the idea of patience from classical Greece to the present is the synoptic review of primary texts offered by M. Spanneut in *Dictionnaire de Spiritualite Ascetique et Mystique, Doctrine et Histoire*, A. Rayez, A. Derville and A. Solignac, SJ, eds. (Paris: Beauchesne, 1984) vol. 12, part 1, cols. 438-476. A useful abbreviated bibliography can also be

found in Gerald J. Schiffhorst, SJ, ed., *The Triumph of Patience* (Orlando: University Presses of Florida, 1978), 36-64.

CHAPTER TWO

1. Norman H. Snaith, *The Distinctive Ideas of the Old Testament* (London: The Epworth Press, 1944), 102. For a study of the ways that persistence and other varieties of patience appear in the Bible, see companion articles by W. Meikle, "The Vocabulary of 'Patience' in the Old Testament" and "The Vocabulary of 'Patience' in the New Testament," in *The Expositor*, 8th series, vol. 19, W. Robertson Nicoll, ed. (London: Hodder and Stoughton, 1920), 219-225 and 304-313.
2. Karl Barth, *Church Dogmatics*, vol. 2, pt. 1, G. W. Bromiley and T. F. Torrance, eds. (Edinburgh: T. and T. Clark, 1957), 413.
3. *Ibid.*, 409-410.
4. *Ibid.*, 432.

CHAPTER THREE

1. Cyprian, *The Good of Patience*, bk. 7.
2. Seneca, *On Anger*, 2.12.6.
3. Lactantius, *The Divine Institutes*, 6.17-18.
4. *Ibid.*, 5.22.
5. Tertullian, *Patience*, 1.7.
6. *Ibid.*, 3.1; 3.10; 4.5.
7. *Ibid.*, 12.10, 8; 1.1; 11.6.
8. *Ibid.*, 13.2.
9. *Ibid.*, 10.2; 8.8; 7.1.
10. *Ibid.*, 5.3; 5.7; 5.15, 18; 5.20-21.
11. Cyprian, *Good of Patience*, bks. 4; 8.
12. *Ibid.*, bk. 10.
13. *Ibid.*, bk. 19.

14. *Ibid.*, bks. 20; 15.
15. Augustine, *On Patience*, ch. 2.
16. *Ibid.*, chh. 4-5; 11; 9.
17. *Ibid.*, chh. 14; 12.
18. Augustine, *On the Gift of Perseverance*, chh. 4, 5, 6.
19. *Ibid.*, chh. 7, 8, 9.

CHAPTER FOUR

1. Gregory the Great, *Morals on the Book of Job*, 1.Preface.14.
2. *Ibid.*, 1.Epistle.5.
3. *Ibid.*, 1.2.9.32.
4. *Ibid.*, 2.4.21.33-34.
5. *Ibid.*, 1.1.5.32-33.
6. Gregory the Great, *Homiliarum in Exechielem Prophetam* 2.35.col. 1261D.
7. Gregory the Great, *Pastoral Care*, 3.9.
8. Thomas Aquinas, *Summa Theologica*, 2.123.3; 2.123.6; 2.123.2; Etienne Gilson, *The Christian Philosophy of St. Thomas Aquinas*, L. K. Shook, CSB, trans. (London: Victor Gollancz, 1957), 289.
9. Thomas Aquinas, *Summa*, 2.128.1. In *After Virtue* (London: Gerald Duckworth, 1981) Alasdair MacIntyre contends that "it is worth picking out some central features of Aquinas' treatment of the virtues which make of Aquinas an unexpectedly marginal figure in the history which I am writing....There is first of all his...exhaustive and consistent classificatory scheme. Such large classificatory schemes ought always to arouse our suspicions" (166). MacIntyre is entirely correct. The annexation of lesser to principal virtues is not consistently persuasive: there is no way that many versions of patience as forbearance and expectant waiting can be related principally to courage. The small virtue is frequently much more closely related to justice as well as to temperance and prudence.

10. *Ibid.*, 2.136.4.
11. *Ibid.*, 2.136.3.
12. Thomas à Kempis, *The Imitation of Christ*, 2.12.1ff.
13. Thomas à Kempis, *Vera Sapientia or True Wisdom*, Frederick Byrne, trans. (London: R. and T. Washbourne, 1904), 143; *Imitation*, 3.19.4; 3.18.1-3.
14. Thomas à Kempis, *Imitation*, 2.12.11; 2.12.4-5.
15. Thomas à Kempis, *True Wisdom*, 139.
16. Thomas à Kempis, *Imitation*, 1.16.4.
17. *Ibid.*, 3.41.1-2.
18. *Ibid.*, 1.16.2.
19. *Ibid.*, 3.57.3; 3.7.1
20. Thomas à Kempis, *True Wisdom*, 144.

CHAPTER FIVE

1. Jonathan Edwards, *Charity and its Fruits* (London: The Banner of Truth Trust, 1969), 292; 295-296.
2. John Calvin, *Institutes of the Christian Religion*, 1.16.3.
3. *Ibid.*, 1.17.2.
4. *Ibid.*, 1.17.8.
5. *Ibid.*, 3.8.9.
6. *Ibid.*, 3.3.3-9.
7. *Ibid.*, 3.7.1; John Calvin, *Commentary on Matthew* (16:24), quoted in Ronald S. Wallace, *Calvin's Doctrine of the Christian Life* (Edinburgh: Oliver and Boyd, 1959), 53; Calvin, *Institutes*, 1.16.2.
8. Calvin, *Institutes*, 3.7.10.
9. *Ibid.*, 3.8.1.
10. *Ibid.*, 3.8.4.
11. *Ibid.*, 3.10.6.
12. *Ibid.*, 3.20.1; 3.20.50.
13. *Ibid.*, 2.3.11-12; 3.24.6.

14. Jeremiah Burroughs, *The Rare Jewel of Christian Contentment* (London: The Banner of Truth Trust, 1964), 19; 41.
15. *Ibid.*, 59; 45.
16. *Ibid.*, 36; 20; 21.
17. *Ibid.*, 120-121.
18. *Ibid.*, 6; 68; 122-123; 132.
19. *Ibid.*, 154; 204.
20. *Ibid.*, 217.
21. Søren Kierkegaard, *Purity of Heart*, Douglas V. Steere, ed. and trans. (New York: Harper and Brothers, 1956), 31; 79.
22. *Ibid.*, 101.
23. *Ibid.*, 103.
24. *Ibid.*, 201.
25. *Ibid.*, 202-203.
26. *Ibid.*, 217-218; 22.
27. Søren Kierkegaard, *Eighteen Upbuilding Discourses*, Howard V. Hong and Edna H. Hong, trans. (Princeton: Princeton University Press, 1990), 115-116.
28. *Ibid.*, 119; 121; 122. Compare the material on Job in Kierkegaard, *Repetition*, Walter Lowrie, trans. (Princeton: Princeton University Press, 1942), esp. 110-134.
29. D. Z. Phillips, *Through A Darkening Glass* (Oxford: Basil Blackwell, Ltd., 1982), 100.
30. Kierkegaard, *Discourses*, 168.

CHAPTER SIX

1. Archibald MacLeish, *J. B.* (Boston: Houghton Mifflin, 1957), 153.
2. *The Oxford Dictionary of English Etymology*, C. T. Onions, ed. (Oxford: Clarendon Press, 1966), s.v. "patience."
3. Martin Luther, *The Small Catechism*, 2.1.
4. Vanstone, *Stature of Waiting*, 31; 13.
5. *Ibid.*, 31.

6. *Ibid.*, 95.
7. *Ibid.*, 83.
8. *Ibid.*, 96.
9. *Ibid.*, 110.
10. *Ibid.*, 115.
11. Iris Murdoch, *The Sovereignty of Good* (London: Routledge, 1970), 34, 37.
12. *Ibid.*, 91.
13. *Ibid.*, 39.
14. Simone Weil, *Waiting for God*, Emma Craufurd, trans. (London: Routledge and Kegan Paul, 1951), 73.
15. Dorothee Soelle, *Suffering*, Everett R. Kalin, trans. (London: Darton Longman & Todd, 1975), 103.
16. Nathan A. Scott, Jr., *The Poetry of Civic Virtue* (Philadelphia: Fortress Press, 1976), 42-43.

CHAPTER SEVEN

1. John Donne, "Meditation XVII," *Devotions Upon Emergent Occasions* (New York: Oxford University Press, 1987), 87.
2. Søren Kierkegaard, *Either/Or*, vol. 1, David F. Swenson and Lillian Marvin Swenson, trans. (Princeton: Princeton University Press, 1971), 282-283.
3. *Ibid.*, 287-288.

CHAPTER EIGHT

1. Matthew Arnold, "Dover Beach," *The Portable Matthew Arnold* (New York: Viking, 1949).
2. *Oxford English Dictionary*, s.v. "humility."
3. C. S. Lewis, *The Screwtape Letters* (New York: New American Library, 1988), 54.
4. *Ibid.*, 54-55.

5. MacIntyre, in *After Virtue,* comments: "The New Testament not only praises virtues of which Aristotle knows nothing—faith, hope and love—and says nothing about virtues such as *phronesis,* which are crucial for Aristotle, but it praises at least one quality as a virtue which Aristotle seems to count as one of the vices relative to magnanimity, namely humility. Moreover since the New Testament quite clearly sees the rich as destined for the pains of Hell, it is clear that the key virtues cannot be available to them; yet they *are* available to slaves" (170). It must be stressed, however, that what defines the rich is not the number of their possessions but, as Augustine tells us, their pride and sense of self-sufficiency, the absence of a sense of dependence and thankfulness.
6. *The New English Hymnal* (Norwich: The Canterbury Press, 1986), no. 73.

EPILOGUE

1. Percy Bysshe Shelley, "Ozymandias," *John Keats and Percy Bysshe Shelley: Complete Poetical Works* (New York: The Modern Library, 1955).